Memory in the Cells

Memory
in the Cells

LUIS ANGEL DIAZ

iUniverse, Inc.
Bloomington

MEMORY IN THE CELLS
HOW TO HEAL OUR BEHAVIORAL PATTERNS

iUniverse books may be ordered through booksellers or by contacting:

iUniverse
1663 Liberty Drive
Bloomington, IN 47403
www.iuniverse.com
1-800-Authors (1-800-288-4677)

ISBN: 978-0-595-52378-8 (sc)
ISBN: 978-0-595-62435-5 (ebk)

Printed in the United States of America

iUniverse rev. date: 09/29/2010

Contents

ACKNOWLEDGMENTS

This book is for you Adriana, my friend and life partner, with whom we created the things I value the most in my life: our three children, Maria, Magdalena and Santiago and this powerful work that has allowed me to meet beautiful friends everywhere I go.

Also, I want to acknowledge:

Silvia de Rojas from Argentina, for her valuable help in putting together the spanish edition.

Savannah Hansen and Pamela Astarte for their unconditional support editing the english one.

Finally, Luis Arturo Martinez from Mexico, for al the graphics you see in this book.

FOREWORD
Arjuna Ardagh

To begin, I must confess that the way I am writing this foreword to Luis Diaz's book involves a kind of cheating. Usually the foreword is written just on the merits of the book alone. In this case I have access to background information that gives me an unfair handicap. I have known the author quite well for many years. We have been in a mens' group together, we swim in the South Yuba River together, we eat food together, we take walks here in the Sierra Nevada Mountains.

I've met so many people over the years who have written great books, with great methods, but the question always arises, "How much is what they are writing about reflected in the way they live?"

Someone could, for example, write a book about emotional freedom, but how does he or she actually respond when insulted? Somebody else could write a book about success and trust, but how much is that reflected in the way that person deals with life's little disappointments? That is always the question when it comes to a book. It all sounds good, but how much is it lived? And this is where my cheating can be helpful to me and to you, the reader, as well, because this book is not just a theory of releasing memory from the cells. This book is written by somebody who is palpably living in a released way. Just from the way that he chooses to spend his time, or just how he is with a waitress in the restaurant, or with his kids, you can feel that this is a book written not only from a theory, but from a different way of perceiving life.

This an important thing, because we are often in the habit of turning to people for advice who do not necessarily have mastery in what we want to know about. About a year ago, I went to a conference where a celibate nun from India was giving a lecture. A young woman at the event stood up to ask a question, "I'd like to get some advice. I'm a new mother. I'd like your direction on how I can raise my daughter." The celibate nun then gave a five-minute lecture about raising children. I asked myself, "What's wrong with this picture?" If you want advice about raising children, the last person in the world to ask is a celibate nun from India. But this is what we do. We follow the words of a renunciate teacher about money, we follow the teachings of someone who's never been in a relationship about relationships. So easily we look for our answers in all the wrong places.

The beautiful thing about this book is that it is not just words, it is written by somebody who has actually passed through and come out the other side of the journey he is inviting you to take, and is still practicing.

There are several things I want to share with you that make this book worthy of your time and set it apart from similar works.

First, it offers freedom from the mind, rather than comfort within the mind. Over many decades now, there has been a growing understanding that we are affected by our thoughts and our beliefs. This understanding started with Napoleon Hill's *Think and Grow Rich*, and came to a crescendo of popularity with the movie *The Secret*. Suddenly everybody understood that what you think creates your life, so if you change your thoughts, you can change your life. That seems very logical—it is obviously true, isn't it? If somebody thinks negative and depressed thoughts all the time, good things do not generally happen to him or her. Somebody who's very happy and positive generally has good things happen. So we come to the predictable conclusion, "Okay, so I should have happy thoughts. If I have happy thoughts, then I'll have a happy life." This seems very logical, but there is also a limit to this way of thinking. The Russian philosopher George Gurdeiff once said, "Human beings live in a prison cell of their own creation. And almost everybody is content to rearrange the furniture in their prison cell and to call it freedom." Almost every book, every approach, every teacher who speaks about limiting belief, will tell you that you need to change your negative beliefs into positive beliefs to create a happy life. This is what Gurdieff calls rearranging the furniture in the prison cell. It has two primary limitations. First, if you are living primarily within the limits of the mind, of thinking, it means that you are cut off from a much, much greater source of creativity and power. And the second thing is that belief always works in polarity, so if you get very attached to positive beliefs, you've actually got a bungee cord attached to negative beliefs as well. The more you hang on to the idea "I am wealthy and loved and in perfect health," the more a charge, or fear, is reinforced in poverty, loneliness, and disease.

The book that you hold in your hand is a rare example of an emerging breed of understanding, one which I call "translucent." The word translucent means not completely opaque and not completely transparent. A piece of stained glass, for example, when you shine light on it, seems to glow. It lets light pass though it, but it retains its quality.

You could say that a human being or an approach becomes translucent when it allows light to pass through it. What Luis is guiding you to in this book is not how to change your beliefs, but how to actually get free of the realm in which belief arises. In this way, your life may in fact get better, you may get the results that you want. This does not happen by trying to change the negative to the positive. It happens by recognizing the vast ground of being in which all beliefs are arising.

Second, this book bridges the gap which has been very prevalent between material well-being and spiritual awakening. We have tended to either work with techniques to make our life better, or to relax and let go into the mysterious, mystical ground of being that we can awaken. This little book will give you the practical tools to not only change the quality of your mind, but to be free of your mind at the same time. It bridges the schism between spirit and having a functional, happy life with flowing relationships, money, and health. When we start to practice the kind of work that Luis is teaching, we discover that the bridging of this gap between awakening and material functionality actually brings fulfillment to both sides of the gap. We discover that you can't actually have a real, functional life without being connected to the source of life, without awakening. And you can't really be connected to the source of life if your physical life is in a mess, because it's going to keep distracting you.

This book is an example of the emergence of a new kind of synthesis, a new kind of integration, which helps us to see that the gap we've made between spirit and the body, between awakening and material well-being, between universal love and functional relationships has really been to our detriment. This book will give you the tools to actually bring all of that into one integrated opening.

Third, in a very practical way, this book focuses on what actually makes a difference. Luis likes to tell the story of a small town or village whose water supply has become contaminated by some kind of fungus. He suggests that two experts are called in to assess the situation. One recommends to pour more and more clean water into the reservoir, so as to drown out the contaminated water with fresh water. The other expert suggests to treat and eliminate the fungus, and that then clean water will be permanently restored. With a mischievous twinkle in his eye, Luis likes to ask his students which approach sounds more effective. Of course, almost everyone prefers the second one. We all want to be happy, we want to have good relationships, we want to make money, we want good health. So we tend to focus on how to get those things. But all those things come naturally when we just pay attention to what is in the way. It is your birthright to have a loving relationship. It's your birthright to have a flow of enough, a feeling of satisfaction. It's your birthright to have good health. What is important is to see and release what is in the way. Luis never loses sight of your full potential in this book; he offers you a way to see that it is the blocks in the way that need our attention, the rest will happen on its own. So this gives you a systematic, reliable way to experience and to dissolve the pain body without getting caught in the story of who did what to who and when and why.

Fourth, this book will restore your trust in the body's natural wisdom. Just as it is the body that has stored our pain, so it is also the body that has a natural intelligence. If you can tune in to and trust that intelligence, the body will unravel its own pain and come back into its natural state. This is an approach that finds that perfect balance between neither getting lost in the story (which is the trap of a lot of psychotherapy) nor denying the story (which is the trap of a lot of spiritual teachings), but actually trusting the intelligence of the body to be able to throw off what it no longer needs.

Luis will show you that the contractions in the body are all created by our unconscious belief systems. If we believe "I'm alone and nobody loves me," or "everything's difficult and I won't be able to make it," or "I'm lost," these are distortions of perception. When we distort things in this way, the life force contracts. These contractions become our suffering. This is an approach that integrates our experience in the mind as beliefs, and in the body as physical contractions. Luis recognizes that we are completely unconscious of some of these blocks because it is a pain that we have been given when we were very young or it was passed to us in our DNA when we were embryos. We are so unconscious of them that we just replay them.

And lastly, this little book will help you to do something so brave and unusual and transformative that I can't imagine why I left it to the last. Luis will help you to make friends with your pain, and even to welcome pain as a friend and teacher. You are probably asking yourself, "What did you say? Why on earth would I want to do *that*?" All the great spiritual teachings have told us that "we are powerful, we are freedom, we are love." And one might legitimately reply, "Okay, that is fine, but what about all these contractions? I am full of contractions over here!" The contractions remain contracted until they are felt, welcomed, embraced. As soon as we turn to meet them with genuine embrace, they start to open up, and then natural joy and freedom and openness start to flow through us again.

We are programmed to believe that pain is bad, that pain is wrong, it is *someone's fault*. If we can't find someone else to blame, we blame ourselves, we blame God, we blame life. Pain becomes the bad guy in the movie. When we don't know the hidden treasure it conceals, we just run from it. Pain has a message for us, a gift for us, an initiation into something deeper. If you are willing to walk into the pain, it becomes a blessing.

I started this little foreword with a confession that it is cheating. But there is another level of cheating as well that I have not yet confessed. Since the early '70s, I have received and trained in many, many approaches to liberation, some have worked well and some have not. So there are very few things that I'm really willing to subject myself to these days. Not only have I taken walks with Luis, and eaten together, and watched movies late into the night, I have also asked him to guide me in his process of CMR. I trust him. Luis has skillfully guided me back into pockets of pain that I had thought were long since left behind, and has midwifed a much deeper and more complete integration.

This approach is for real, it is effective and brilliant, and it comes to you from a man of unusual integrity and fullness of heart.

Read on and enjoy!

Arjuna Ardagh
author of The Translucent Revolution and seven other books
awakeningcoachingtraining.com

SPANISH EDITION FOREWORD

The pain body release (PBR) process is part of the cellular memory release (CMR) synthesis for transformation that leads us to find our full human potential. From a creative intelligence and the opening of his heart, Luis Angel Diaz has given us the gift of these pages so that we can begin to work with this method for inner transformation and healing. This is the path to discovering our real possibilities of expansion and our true light essence, peace and love. As a path, it provides further opportunities to open doors leading to ever more remote places, forgotten memories, and deeper levels of awareness. It is as if a waterfall of free associations opens many remote and forgotten experiences that, though interrelated, we probably have never had access to before.

I was surprised by the similarity of this process with that of the psychoanalytic experience that I know so well. Indeed, while in psychoanalysis the aim is making conscious the unconscious through so-called "free associations" and interpretations, in CMR the way is through the "pain body," a term that summarizes the entire gamut of human suffering. In this model of intervention, we cross through ever deeper layers of experiences not yet assimilated or integrated that have been perhaps stagnated in our physical body and are frozen in our emotional body like indelible, and often invisible, marks.

I wish to underline the speed of the intervention and the results obtained through this approach, which I consider one of its invaluable virtues. In the brief time of an hour and a half of each CMR session, it is possible that the person may return to experiences of her intrauterine life or of her birth. The briefness and depth of this technique is analogous to that of a laser beam.

A French girl adopted by a Canadian family came to see me because she had the obsessive and vehement desire of meeting her natural mother. Because of the events related to her adoption, it was impossible for her to fulfill her desire. During our meeting, it became obvious that she wanted to know the circumstances surrounding her pregnancy, which had left a permanent imprint in her life. She would often express, with a sense of unease and disappointment, that she was "a mistake." I worked with this material using the CMR method and could help her access these deep levels, tracing the feelings she experienced when saying those words. To my surprise, she reached intrauterine experiences in which she felt to be, in her words, "the product of her young parents' mistake." She reported hearing things like, "This pregnancy has been an error in calculation." She also was quite certain that her parents were very young at that time. During one session, she expressed her gratefulness for not having been aborted, empathized with her parents for the difficult time they had had—she said that in similar circumstances, she would have most likely done the same—and was also thankful for having been given up in adoption. After that session, the symptoms for which the girl had come to the consultation eventually disappeared.

Our environment is influenced by all of our feelings and thoughts, however unknown to us they might be. Thus, the unconscious determines our becoming; it is as if it designs our fate without our awareness. Here we have a way to transform the pain body into a light body. This approach allows us to leave behind the heavy burden that binds us so as to embrace the present that liberates us, to go from the victim's passive and subjugated world into the autonomous, responsible world of creative freedom. The resentful experiences are blurred, and thankfulness and gratitude emerge in their place. The delusional world of fear is transformed into the creative world of love. Contracted energy is released and it remains open to further expansion. That which we do not know is disclosed and opened up under the light. New levels of consciousness, integration, realization, fulfillment, and joy are reached.

The book we have in our hands is an enriching opportunity to immerse ourselves in this exciting world of inner liberation. We can only thank Luis Diaz for this invaluable contribution, in keeping with the needs of our time. His message is a gift and a challenge at the same time: to release our cellular memory means to open ourselves to a new way of being and to what we truly are.

Marianella Vallejo Valencia
Psychologist, Family and Couples Psychoanalyst
Bogotá, Colombia, February 2007
neopsicologia1@hotmail.com

CHAPTER 1
Cellular Memory Release

"Freedom, peace, and inner joy will continue to elude us until we become aware of our real truth, without hiding ourselves or being ashamed of what we are."
—Lynn Grabhorn

The Search

It is possible for you to connect with well-being, freedom, and inner peace. It is possible for you to feel in each pore of your skin, fully harmonized with everything around you and with the joy of being alive. Paradoxically, you can also achieve it through physical or emotional pain, touching the bottom of it in order to rise and reach peace, a peace born of acceptance, of reconciling yourself to your own being in communion with the universe.

If you're suffering, you're already on the road. If some part of you somehow knows or feels that there's something else beyond what your senses may perceive, you're already on the road. If you believe that this much suffering in the world must give rise to some kind of awakening, you're already on the road. If you are reading this book, you may start rebuilding the meaning of your life. Perhaps you won't be able to change what is happening to you, but you'll surely be able to change what it causes and means to you.

Remember: there is an incredibly vast intelligence within you, the same that operates in all the universe.

My Background and Life

When I was young, I used to observe adults. Life appeared before my eyes like a motion picture, and it seemed to me that adults were actors and actresses playing out a script and each had a role. When I was five, I had already experienced what I later knew to be called depression. I felt "heavy," unconnected with the world, and had suicidal thoughts. I was overcome by feelings of weakness and helplessness. I was almost always tired. My body became overweight and I constantly avoided the unpleasant feelings it caused by bingeing or watching too much TV. Even at that early age I deeply felt with certitude that, beyond what I saw, there must be another way of living. Beneath a facade of tenderness, efficiency, and adjustment, an enduring emotional pain was germinating within me. Later, when I had been "civilized" and "tamed" by the culture in which I happened to be, that feeling withdrew to the background and it was more or less forgotten. At that point in my life, as it usually happens, I had already learned how to conceal and deny my feelings.

During the long and painful process of becoming an adolescent, I was gradually led to firmly believe that there was some fault, some insurmountable defect in me. This gave rise, however, to confusing and contradictory feelings since I was able to see things differently than the rest of those around me. I could perceive beyond the patterns established by the adults, which made me feel shameful and guilty, but also special. "Who do you think you are?" an increasingly resonant voice kept asking. That inner tension expressed itself in my body through pain in my neck and back, digestive problems, and heartburn. My permanent and intense anxiety and worrying became a chronic silent behavior.

When I was only seventeen, I felt so desperate that I looked for help in psychoanalysis. Together with María Lidia, a gentle professional with a spiritual background, who was neither religious nor dogmatic, I began to acknowledge that I had been lying to myself. I realized that my family's socially accepted values and priorities, such as being somebody in the world or being worried about what other people might think, had never been truly important to me. I also didn't seem to care about creating my own family, having a good reputation, or getting much money as a way of getting a passport to a fruitful life. Thus, at age twenty-one, against the advice of everybody, I gave up studying architecture and I engaged in the practice of yoga, meditation, and vegetarianism in the company of a group of Hindu monks. They taught me many things that would be useful in my career. At the same time, I began studying holistic healing and Eastern medicine. It was a complete radical change that gave birth to a new life of creativity, purpose, and joy, the same life I have today, many years later.

At twenty-one, I was learning one of the most relevant things a human being may learn—namely, to make my own choices based on what made me feel good, instead of making them based on what I should do or what was expected of me. I also learned that to look permanently for the acceptance and approval of others is a perfect formula for suffering, in which one always says "yes" to others and "no" to oneself. From then on, I began a search for the individual liberation all Eastern doctrines promise. I studied and practiced several approaches to healing and to conscious awareness. I took part in innumerable workshops and training courses. I wanted to expand my knowledge, and learn how to improve my life and help others do the same. Thus, I was trained in shiatsu and many other Eastern approaches to health: Chi Kung, Tui na, nutrition, macrobiotics, acupressure, acupuncture, ear therapy, herbal medicine, homeopathy, and reflexology. Driven by the passion to learn more and to be ever more efficient in my work, I also studied scientific astrology, iridology, hypnotherapy, Neuro-Linguistic Programming

(NLP), Touch for Health, specialized kinesiology, Neural Organization Technique (NOT), Emotional Freedom Technique (EFT), and a few other disciplines.

An Unexpected Transformation

With the best aims in mind, I submerged myself for years in the study of several academic and spiritual fields of knowledge linked with my career, and studied several cosmogonies and healing methods. In spite of all that, I still wasn't at peace with myself, and didn't feel free, much less happy. I felt as if I were incomplete. There was always "something" lacking in my life. Some years later, in the most unexpected way, an experience of deep and intense pain such as I had never suffered before, triggered a transformation that I hadn't deemed possible. This seemingly unbearable pain led me to discover something that was to be my guide, though I was hardly aware of it, a presence emanating from my own self and impregnating my whole body. Suddenly, the transformation of my pain permitted me to draw back the veil and I no longer felt the urge to search. I somehow knew that none of my former worries was essentially real to me, and that the kind of life I had so diligently led wasn't either.

At that moment, the original certitude I had had in my childhood was rescued from oblivion and I understood with all my being that the world I had thought real wasn't real at all. I experienced a sense of fullness for the first time, and with that realization I achieved a sense of liberation and a profound feeling of peace that still is my guide in the present.

The Creation of Cellular Memory Release (CMR)

My interest in studying cellular memory began when I was about thirty years old and deepened eight years later, when Adriana—my wife and companion, and mother of my three children—suddenly died. When

Adriana and I had lunch in Sausalito one sunny day before I left for a trip to South America, I had no way to know I would never see her conscious again. While I was gone, she fainted and then went into a deep coma from which she was never to awaken. In the hospital, doctors discovered a brain aneurysm. Sitting next to her in the hospital bed after my frantic return from South America, I was shocked, drowning as if anesthetized by the blow. An inner voice asked over and over again, "Why? Why? Why?" I felt the pressure of a heavy, unbearable iron crown around my head. I couldn't cry. I was frozen, although I managed to stay calm and under control.

I was in the intensive care unit with Kelly, a dear friend and student. She approached me and said, "Well, now we're going to do what you've taught us." I knew at once what she meant. She was referring to the work I was beginning to slowly develop with my students and clients in which we allow ourselves to deeply and fully recognize whatever we are feeling as it arises in our bodies rather than blocking any upset or negative emotions, or getting lost in any thoughts or stories about the experience. I gave in. I stopped thinking and analyzing, I tried to stop controlling my feelings, and I began to accept that I knew absolutely nothing. The permission I gave myself to feel the full extent of the pain raging through my body triggered an "out-of-time" experience that was only a few minutes long, but seemed to last a lifetime. The experience led me to feel an assortment of very intense inner states: denial of what was happening, profound rage, the feeling of having been abandoned, terror of the future, and, paradoxically, also guilt, a lot of guilt.

Adriana eventually was gone, yet somehow her leaving planted the seed of an incredible gift, the gift of awakening to a new life. The shock produced by her loss was the first step in an inner process that completely changed my perception of myself and of my life. I stopped my practice and all my activities for more than six months after Adriana's departure. For that period, my entire world contained only our three children and myself. All during this time I kept journals. I needed to share what was going on within me, yet I couldn't do it. Something in me was telling me to keep it to myself. It was too intimate and very difficult to explain. I didn't know or understand what was going on. For several months I plunged deeper and deeper into physical feelings and sensations, and I began to discover new inner dimensions. Physically, it was as if some parts of me began to open and give me access to places whose existence I had ignored. My body was talking in very unusual ways. Childhood memories that I thought I had forgotten, especially the emotional wounds that were the building blocks of my belief system and my self-image, emerged clearly. Beyond that, I even relived some experiences from intrauterine life, such as the feelings my mother had when she was pregnant. I thought her thoughts and felt how her feelings permeated my being. I also came to know, with absolute certainty, that my training to be the conditioned adult I was had begun in her womb.

But it did not end there. Two years had passed and I was getting more and more used to being present to whatever was arising in me. I was feeling strong in my body and more connected to myself. Several friends told me later that they were wondering what was going on with me since I looked younger and healthier and had lost a lot of weight. I was surprised by a strong need to move and exercise, considering that I had never been fond of any sport or exercise before in my life! I joined a gym and started moving and dancing regularly. This led to an experience that was the most transforming one for me and that marked the beginning of a new life. On a Saturday morning during the fall, I was enjoying my run and sweating on a treadmill when I started having a change in my perception of the moment. I felt as if a veil was unzipped and gradually I was able to see just energy, the energy of things. Meanwhile, I was breathing heavily and running. The matrix that is behind everything I thought was reality was clean and clear in front of my eyes. Meditating in my youth, I was used to having spiritual experiences of sorts. But this time was somehow very different—it was clean and clear, without mystic interpretations, not even emotions. An awareness was there that knew everything about everything. It was just that, being-ness—deep, profound, peaceful being-ness.

Slowly and after a few moments, my thinking mind that had remained deactivated during that entire time, started slowly to come back. I even became aware of its physical location. I could locate it on my right side, six feet or so behind and above my head. It was as though a drop of black ink fell into a glass of pristinely clear water.

I could hear it with a very weak voice, judging the experience that was taking place. "This is not right! This is dangerous! You can't do this!" These three phrases kept coming out from that place and slowly and gradually growing in strength and volume. I began to feel a rush of intense feelings. I felt the grief for myself and for all humanity, for not being able to be in touch with what I had just come to *know as* our most genuine nature. And as the voice from the far right got closer and louder, I started experiencing fear, and then the fear became terror. A deep cramp in my gut made me jump off of the machine and bend myself in two. "This is very dangerous! You are going to lose everything! You are going to lose your health, your reputation, your mind!"

I ran immediately into the men's room and locked myself in the toilet stall. I sat on the toilet contracting in terror and I knew that I was experiencing what is called a panic attack. A command inside me said, "Get out of this. You know how to stop this. Do it now!" At the same time and from another place in myself, I heard, "Feel it deeply and fully." To hear that didn't surprise me. In the last two years I had been gradually becoming used to this diving into the uncomfortable feelings. The terror was increasing as the loud demanding voice was saying, "If you feel this, you will die!"

At that moment the decision was made. "All right, then I will die," I heard myself saying, and then I let myself sink into that big contraction and the feelings of despair and terror.

This fantastic inner journey was warped with fire and smoke; the memories of the emotions were absorbed by intense whirls of energy where they burned. As in a time travel experience, memories of the time I had spent before being in my mother's womb came to me, and I simply felt what I called "human pain," layer upon layer of energy crushed into my being at an enormous pressure, very old memories of generations after generations of my ancestors. I recognized parts of myself that I found repulsive. I discovered places where I didn't want to go at all, and at the same time I knew with utmost clarity that they were precisely the places I had to enter if I wanted to find the way out. I let myself go into and through those places until unexpectedly I had access to a place of complete well-being where I finally felt profoundly at peace, free, and filled with immeasurable love. I was able to acknowledge myself, to know whom, or more precisely what, I was. I realized that before reaching that inner place of acceptance I had been numb and drowsy, as if I had been dead.

I came out of the men's room after an immeasurable amount of time, yet perhaps it was fifteen minutes of clock time—like from outer space, feeling internally very light and very confused at the same time. A newspaper's front page resting on a backpack in the men's locker room said in capital letters, "IT IS ABOUT TIME." Although the headline was supposedly about daylight saving time, I took it as a message for me, gently letting me know that I was not alone. Somehow I felt relieved. To go through that experience for me was like opening inner doors and learning a deeply transforming lesson. I came to know that the process I was experiencing was possible for all human beings and that sooner or later everyone will open those mysterious doors. For the first time since I could remember, I was experiencing deep and profound peace all day long. I hadn't realized how tense and anxious I had been until then. I didn't know that I had so much fear lodged in my body. I also realized that when we feel anxiety we are gradually releasing fear in a civilized, proper way.

This process deepened with time, as did my own peace and self-acceptance. I realized that in spite of having studied and practiced for almost two decades, I didn't know the role pain and negative emotions play in human life. In fact, I knew nothing about pain. It was tragic and comical all at once. I had been struggling all my life against something I didn't understand, and actually this unknown thing was giving me new life! Trained to relieve or eradicate what was painful and uncomfortable, I had fought, resisted, rejected, avoided, and denied pain in myself and in others. I had only learned that pain must be gotten rid of at all costs. Where there is pain, an error has been made. When there is pain, someone is to blame for it. And if the guilty person isn't outside, it must be inside me. To let pain be, to allow myself to make friends with it, was something that had never crossed my mind. I hadn't yet found that miraculous door. And the miracle is possible only through a state of presence that penetrates that thin border where something within us stops to contemplate what happens in the world we call reality.

Adriana's death revealed the map of my inner being and taught me how to travel through that territory. Almost without realizing it, I gradually got used to being present to whatever happens, and accepting it. I knew I had everything I needed, and that everything was potentially within me, waiting to be recognized. I knew that the body is my best ally and that an incredibly vast intelligence permeates it and is activated each time I am present to it. Some years later, I read a book by the Indian spiritual teacher Kabir and I felt his words were the reflection of my own experience. He said, "I felt it for fifteen seconds, and after that I devoted my whole life to serve it." I didn't realize yet that those experiences were what were giving life to the CMR process.

Working with the Pain Body

Months later, when I began to use this same technique with my clients, I noticed that it worked wonderfully. I noticed in my daily consultations

unexpected healings and transformations the likes of which I had never
achieved before. I observed that the layers of stored and accumulated
negative emotional charge may generate many imbalances in body,
mind, and soul. But I also found that human beings are designed to be
able to transform pain, and that to accumulate it as we usually do goes
against that original design condemning us to live in a very limited and
conditioned way. I was able to see that, under the overlapped layers of
compacted, contracted energy there was in each of us an extraordinary
source of vital force, of which my logic and reason could not conceive.
There seemed to be a state of well-being that was difficult to describe.
One could only say that it was an inexplicable mix of a very deep self-
love, a sense of freedom, inner peace, and the joy of living. How could
it be that everyone had this in their inner being and could not access it?
How it could be that we were trying to find it outside ourselves when
we had it at the core of our being?

I suddenly remembered a tale about a beggar in India who sat
daily in the street outstretching his hand to passersby for alms, without
knowing that the box on which he was sitting was full of gold coins! All
of us—the good and the bad, the wise and the ignorant, the spiritual
and the agnostic—have within us this powerful place I call the core
of well-being. It is the power source that makes us what we are and
keeps our bodies alive and vibrant. It is in charge of all of our vital
functions—of movement, the mind, the emotions, growth, self-healing,
and reproduction. As long as we are alive, we have within us this core
of well-being. Every living creature is supported by this power source.
In human beings, it is unfortunately drowned under layer upon layer
of pain, created by energy contractions that separate us from this state
of well-being. In my perception, Jesus Christ speaks of it in this way,
"There is a peace that surpasses all understanding," while the separation
from it is the result of an inner split that gives rise to a dreaming state
that prevents us from clearly seeing what we really are. This state some
spiritual teachings call the dreaming state or illusion, and the Hindu

call it "maya." Immersed in it, we believe the unreal and cannot see the untrue. In some people, the state created by this source of well-being is more available because they have fewer layers of compacted energy, are more aware of the reality of their situation, and can find ways to voluntarily connect themselves with this inner source.

Gates leading to this place are opened when one lets sensations and emotions be at every moment without censoring, observing that "what is, is such as it is." To permit and accept what happens to us does not mean that we like it or we agree with everything that is happening to us. On the other hand, to make an alliance with "what is" stimulates being present to our own life. That state of being goes beyond the present moment and connects us with the matrix supporting all that exists. When we react and resist what is happening, we are not present. We filter everything through the artificial image we have been told about life and how things should be. Instead, when we are present, we make an alliance with life, and then the whole of creation makes sense and befriends us.

CHAPTER 2
All Is Energy

"The main cause of suffering is ignorance."
—Buddha

You see, Life is intelligent. Life is all-powerful. Life is always, everywhere, trying to express itself. Indeed, it's never satisfied but constantly searching for a larger and fuller expression. The moment a tree stops growing, it searches everywhere new forms of better expression. The moment you stop expressing further and further Life, the Life Force begins to look for newer and better outlets around it.
—Anonymous

We Are Made of Pure Energy

During the years that I was studying and practicing holistic medicine, I came to see a human being as a web of energy, containing all kinds of information. This micro web we call a person is not separate from the macro field of all energy that is life itself, but it can also stagnate into blocked emotional charges. Over the years, the repeated storage of these charges in compacted layers depletes our vital energy, and causes us to feel cut off from the rest of life. The word "emotion" comes from the Latin *emovere*, which means "movement." The suppression of an emotion prevents the natural movement of vital energy. Repression leads to stagnation and paralysis in some part of the human's energy field and, as a result, in the organic systems feeding upon it. When not processed, painful experiences suffocate and reduce the positive emotional charge, leading to a dysfunction in the body-mind system. Throughout our life, we use a large amount of vital force in order to suppress emotions and keep the negative emotional charge at bay. It is like spending large amounts of money in renting a big storage unit to keep toxic useless stuff in it. What would happen if we stop the rental agreement and we decide to get rid of all that stuff? What would happen if we had available all that vital energy used in suppressing negative emotions? What if we could release all that charge stagnated in our cells?

To release the charge is not the same as deleting the memory of the events; it involves liberating the trapped vital force in order to use it for growth and self-healing. The universe is made up entirely of energy. Everything happens within the energy field of the universe, and all that exists is part of it. In the last decades, science has demonstrated what many teachings of old cultures have been saying for thousands of years—namely, that what we call the physical world or the manifest universe is not made up of solid matter, but of energy as its basic component. The entire universe is made up entirely of that energy. Time and space are the dimensions along which that energy moves. Everything we know is composed of energy, in the form of either matter or radiation. One of the most striking characteristics of energy is its ability to remain constant. Until now, the creation or destruction of energy could not be observed or proven. Thus, energy is the fundamental principle that gave origin to the universe, as it has all the needed qualities for this purpose.

The things we see, smell, taste, hear, and touch seem to be solid, liquid, or gaseous, and also seem to be separate. Quantum physics allows us to observe them minutely and in much more detail, in their atomic and subatomic levels. At those levels, what seems to be solid, liquid, or gaseous matter becomes a group of ever smaller particles that are within other even smaller particles, and so on and so forth, until one realizes that everything is simply pure energy. Quantum physics has discovered that even the most dense and solid element, when analyzed to an infinitesimal level, is not what it appears to be. Scientists subscribing to the new paradigm affirm that any visible or touchable element, when reduced to the level of its particles, is no more or no less than 99.99 percent empty space. The notion that an element or object has a given position, mass, or speed is then the result of a false perception. In brief, any created object is an energy vortex largely composed of empty space and of particles whose state cannot be determined, since they are constantly coming into existence or going out of it.

Now, since we are part of that universe and are also made up of fluctuating and changing energy, everything within us—and around us—has that same quality of energy. We are part of an immense sea of energy that is constantly changing and pulsating between a state of existence and nonexistence. If all is energy, and this energy has a different density according to the frequency in which it vibrates, then our thoughts, which are a relatively light and subtle form of energy, are a speedy and easily changeable energy form. A stone, on the other hand, is made up of a relatively much more dense energy and is therefore less likely to be changed.

EXERCISE

1. Now, stop a while to perceive your body and the things surrounding it, and become aware that your body is alive. You don't need to move your legs or your arms to recognize that they are alive. Just feel their presence there. Gradually do the same with some other parts of your body. The cells of your body have been alive all this time while you were reading and thinking.

Your body has been alive and functioning since day one without you noticing it.

2. Take time to realize that there is an incredible intelligence that operates your body and the bodies of all creatures in creation.

3. Breathe deeply while you become more and more aware of these facts. All is energy manifested in different forms and in different states and frequencies.

4. Close your eyes and imagine that you are submerged in a vast ocean of energy. Let yourself be part of it. Breathe, while you recognize that you are alive.

The Light Body and the Original Resonance

In the early stage of our life, when we are infants, we cannot communicate with words, we lack teeth with which to process food, we go through our day with a diaper containing our wastes, and we do not know how to walk. We depend on other people to lead us from one place to the other, to feed us, and to protect us. We are extremely fragile and vulnerable. Even so, we are happy. So let's imagine, for a moment, how our adult life would be if we had to tolerate all of those limitations, or even half of them, or just one. Who of us would not be in despair?

In our first few months of life, even though we are suffering and coping with all those "disabilities," we're charming and lovely beings. At that age, our nature is only to give and receive love; we are innocent, spontaneous, and able to be true to ourselves at every moment. We feel free to ask for and reject anything, any event, even any person. We feel as we feel, without any remorse or shame. Through all history and in all cultures, every infant has come into this world resonating with that joy, love, and freedom. And the same can happen in the future, because that original resonance is our trademark. We call this our light body. It is unconditioned in all of us, as well as in most creatures. This is our birthright. We are naturally a light body with nothing to conceal and nothing to be ashamed about.

When we remind our workshop participants of this, the same question is always asked: "What has happened to us?" How is it possible that, being designed in this way, humans have eventually come to live like they do? There are probably many ways to explain it, but here I'll only mention the conclusions I reached while working with the cell memory within us. The original resonance of the infant called the light body is as malleable as clay before being fired. The baby adapts to every outer stimuli or impression—for instance, to life experiences with the family members or the people with whom she happens to live. Everything begins in our mother's womb. There isn't any more intimate relationship than the one we have with our mother before being born. We felt comfortable and protected during those nine months, if our mother wanted us. It seems difficult to conceive of a more pleasant place, a place we recognize as ours, which is a wonderful feeling of well-being. In this natural state of comfort our body is created. While in gestation, we remain open and absorb everything, and what is given reaches us effortlessly and unconditionally.

To this blessed state, the particular impressions of each pregnancy are added. The infant feels and experiences as hers everything the mother feels. It couldn't be otherwise, since she is within the mother's energy field. Indeed, that period of primary and essential training establishes the emotional patterns and the different kinds of behavior that the gestating being is going to develop while growing up. Any outer or inner change affecting the mother will somehow result in a kind of learning.

> "The development of the fetus is determined by our emotions. Parents are 'genetic engineers.' They transmit to the fetus human emotions such as fear, anger, love, and hope. A human being's personality is determined beginning in the womb."
> —Bruce Lipton, Ph.D.

The fact that the mother's womb is a warm, emotionally rich environment can make a big difference in all of the child's feelings, hopes, emotions, dreams, and thoughts throughout her life. For centuries, many mothers have known through their own experience and intuition that the forthcoming baby feels pain and has emotions, and this has been proven by recent research. Lodged within the uterus is an extremely sensitive individual—first a fetus, then a child—able to hear and feel much of what the mother hears and feels. Thomas Verny, the author of *The Secret Life of the Unborn Child*, is a psychiatrist who has been a pioneer in the field of prenatal psychology. His book is a collection of very valuable research proving that the baby, even while she is in the womb, has a very deep relationship with her parents and the outer world. Furthermore, prenatal psychologists remark that the "center of gravity" of human personality is built up in the womb. It has been observed that just as the baby gets what the mother inhales, eats, or drinks, the mother's thoughts and emotions are also conveyed to the baby. It has also been noted that stress hormones, such as adrenaline, travel through the mother's bloodstream and produce in the baby the same emotional state. Patterns of chronic anxiety, worry, or ambivalence about having or not having the baby may predispose the latter in such a way that she will repeat these same patterns in her future life.

From birth on, the baby is very sensitive to outer influences and responsive to smooth, gentle, and loving contact, while she reacts badly to flashing lights, noises, and the metallic environment associated with birth in medical settings. The mother's ability to remain calm and communicate with her baby during pregnancy, as well as the building of an appropriate environment for a relaxed birth full of love, will immensely contribute to the child's physical and mental health for the rest of her life.

Our Early Programming

We come to the world already designed to absorb indiscriminately the mental and emotional features and patterns of the people who surround us. The love we feel for them is so deep and comprehensive that we wish to merge with them and have them with us all the time. During our baby stage, we don't filter anything, we simply receive. Why would we, especially if we feel permeated with love and it felt good for nine months? However, while the need to experience that loving, intimate well-being is constant (and persists even in adulthood), life outside the womb feels like a perpetual experience of separation, opposite to that of intrauterine life, to the point that we may feel this separation as something intensely uncomfortable or painful.

Everything not felt by the baby as pleasant gives rise to feelings and sentiments of discomfort, which in turn generate responses such as rejection and crying. In that way, through her daily experiences of separation, the baby "learns" that to be open, permeable, and vulnerable is painful, and that one should "close down" to protect oneself. In order to protect herself, she must pretend to not feel what she feels, or should even act as if she feels something that she doesn't feel. That is, she must "perform" and leave behind her authentic way of being. That baby that spontaneously took in what she liked and rejected what she didn't like becomes a child who begins to say "yes" when wanting to say "no." Unaware of this, she begins building a mask that grows more dense and thick with time. The expanding and trusting light body draws back and contracts, and with each contraction an energy field with very different resonances emerges: the resonances of the uncomfortable and painful pain body.

Unfortunately, not even the most loving and understanding family environment can prevent this process of contraction from taking place. Wherever she goes, the baby confronts the unavoidable experience of separation. She will then be given a name that ascribes an identity to her and will be treated as someone who is different from all the rest. If the unconditional merging and the utmost intimacy of the womb gave us love, trust, and inner peace, separation will give us the opposite: mistrust, unrest, pain, and fear. The more intense pain the baby experiences, the deeper the pain is felt—first as the child and then as the adult. This pain will cause emotional wounds that will not heal, because that baby or small child will go on experiencing separation in a world where everybody in her surroundings suffers in the same way, not knowing how to heal either. Consequently, the more the child experiences separation, the more she closes up and hurts herself.

As a rule, human beings want "to feel well"—that is, happy, loving, creative, free, and at peace. We want to have delicious intimate relationships in which to grow together, to give and take unconditionally. Actually, we are unconsciously attempting to relive our early intrauterine experiences of unconditional love and pleasure that rightfully belongs to us by the mere fact of having been born. But though we have a right to it and we have been created for that, we are very deeply afraid of being unconditionally vulnerable, because when we have been innocent and trusting, we suffered so much. That's why the mask, in spite of being uncomfortable and not letting us be what we really are, becomes a useful way to protect us from our earliest painful experiences.

Now, as it happens, not being authentic causes us a profound feeling of self-betrayal that is very distressing and gives rise to the physical, emotional, and spiritual pain we feel. Lived as a contraction in our energy field, this pain makes up the "pain body." At this point, we come to an important crossroads that has been and will be our biggest challenge, and one that we must face and resolve sooner or later: how to live without contraction and recover the light body. The experience I have with my clients—and my own experience—has proven that we are able to recover the light body and be like children again. This process I have termed Cellular Memory Release (CMR) and it has been designed to guide us in un-learning that which causes us pain, and which moves us away from our authentic and true self. In other words, it has been designed to help us transform the contraction of the pain body into a light body, using pain itself to accomplish this.

CHAPTER 3
Opposed and Complementary Frequencies

"The human being is like a hostel.
Each morning a new guest comes by.
This one is joy, this other one is sadness.
There comes meanness,
There comes a spark of awareness.
Dark thoughts, shame, evil.
You can find them at the door, laughing.
Tell them to come in.
Be thankful with those who come
Because each one has been sent
As a guide from beyond."
—Rumi

Everything Is in the Energy Field

I've come to the conclusion ever more deeply through the years that we are inevitably made of the same stuff as all creation. All my work has been devoted to helping others and myself heal our inner fragmentation. In light of this, we must become fuller and more alive human beings, aware that inside we are as incredibly vast and marvelous as the surrounding universe.

Allow yourself to realize, for just one moment, that we are made of energy, pure energy. In the last fifty years scientific research from many different disciplines, especially quantum physicists, has proven that matter and energy are different manifestations of one indivisible energy field. These findings have been published in peer reviewed scientific journals, and popularized for the rest of the world in books like *The Tao of Physics* and *The dancing Wu Li Masters*. Micro Biologists, like Bruce Lipton, have also demonstrated that the cells which constitute the human body, when viewed at the atomic level, are no more than swirling patterns of energy. When we observe the subatomic particles which make up what we call matter, 99.99 percent of it is simply empty space. No matter how dense the object being studied is, it is largely empty space.

> In this universe, everything is energy, and each of us is a particle of it. Awareness makes the difference between understanding this or not. It's as if each particle gave each other a conspiratorial wink, saying, "We know we're the same, but let's make believe we don't know each other."

This discovery has a profound impact on the understanding of whom or what we actually are. It is clear that when we realize with all our being that we are energy in different states of manifestation our self-experience changes radically. This should not come as a surprise. Around 70 percent of our body is water (the same proportion as the Earth), and 85 percent of our brain and nervous system is also water. Water has very high electrical conductivity, and so it is understandable that energy changes can happen quickly within us, sometimes without our being aware of them at all. For instance, while you're reading these words, your body is conducting thousands of physiological actions without making any mistake whatsoever. Your glands and their hormone secretions, your breath, your heartbeat, the circulation of your blood, the digestion of different kinds of food, the cleaning and defense system of the organism all work in unison, silently, without the need of your attention or intention.

Take a moment to consider this: your thoughts are generating storms of info-energy in your brain and nervous system, all at the same time, producing energy movements in your whole body-mind system. In my work, I've also observed that our energy field is able to change very rapidly, since it's the result of the dynamic combination of an infinite amount of elements making up our thoughts, feelings, and sentiments at any given moment. Our energy field may change instantly, affecting our mental activity as well as our physiology and emotional responses. Our state of being is a collective response to thoughts, feelings, and emotions at any given instant. This state of being is what determines, at each and every moment, that which we internally feel and also our external behavior. That's why a change in any of the three component elements (thought, feeling, and emotion) will give rise to many potential combinations and produce diverse kinds of behaviors.

To make it easier to understand, we could compare the human energy field with the bubble surrounding us, which we call biosphere or aura. It includes, among other elements, all the beliefs and inner decisions that condition our behavior, as well as information that comes from past generations. All this material continually stimulates sensations and emotions, generating in our biosphere a certain energy field that we call resonance, which is unique for each individual. If we get used to "feeling bad," this resonance will attract new painful experiences similar to those of the original frequency, leading to further negative beliefs and decisions that will attract more pain, and so forth. Thus, though the experiences and persons may seem to be different, we'll go on vibrating at the same frequency. So, resonances create an imaginary personal picture we call "false self" or "false self-image" that "hangs" before us preventing us from seeing reality "such as it is," like a smoke screen distorting everything. Reality will continue to be altered for us because of the frequency of these resonances.

From a metaphysical point of view, there are universal laws that constantly operate within us generating these patterns. One of these laws is known as the law of attraction. According to it, there are past beliefs and attitudes determining an energy resonance in the present that attracts to us "more of the same" and leads us unconsciously to repeat the same mental or emotional patterns. For instance, if I felt rejected when I was a child, there will be an unconscious resonance of self-rejection and I'll become an artificially amiable person in order to be approved by others and thus avoid the possibility of being rejected again. I'll then go through life saying "yes" when in fact I want to say "no." It will be difficult for me to set limits, I'll often feel used or abused, and I will hold resentful feelings toward others as well as toward myself, generating in turn ever more inner rejection. In that way, the resonance increases and grows in strength indefinitely.

Between Pain and Joy: the Pendulum

Our existence is like a pendulum oscillating between comfortable and uncomfortable states, or, to put it simpler, between pain and joy. To understand this in a more practical way, we can remember that we are no more than swirling patterns of energy. The vital force forming and animating us is very subtle and its state changes continuously. For several decades now, scientists have shared the view that matter and energy are the same thing and, consequently, all is energy and all vibrates within us in a given frequency.

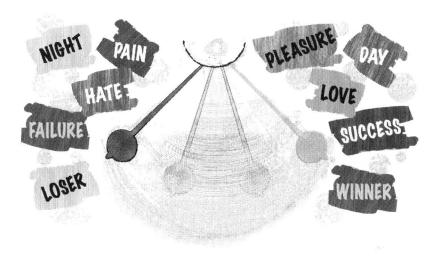

Thousands of years ago, the spiritual teachings of enlightened Hindu sages were carried over to China by teachers traveling from Tibet. They organized and shaped the corpus of knowledge that we now call Eastern philosophy. Fundamental concepts from many of these esoteric teachings have reached us over the centuries and have been patiently elaborated and conveyed to us. In China, for instance, Taoist teachers exposed in a very simple way their theory about the creation of the universe. According to them, before creation there was a primal omnipresent state called "the One Principle." It included the All and the Nothing with all the latent potential of creation. Afterward, the One Principle divided itself into two energy frequencies of equal power but of opposite, complementary nature, called by these sages "yin" and "yang." After that division, the whole creation took place: earth and sky, moon and sun, night and day, male and female, cold and heat, darkness and light, expansion and contraction, low-pitched and high-pitched sounds, etc. From then on, the yin-yang theory was applied to everything, known or unknown. None of these extremes can exist without the other. To recognize the light we must know darkness, to recognize coldness we must experience heat. Similarly, in the Old

Testament, specifically in Genesis, there is a more dramatic and poetic version of the yin-yang theory, when an all-powerful, omnipotent God (the One Principle) creates everything, including man (yang) and woman (yin), and entrusts them to inhabit the Earth and reproduce themselves (giving rise to all the rest).

If we apply to emotional states this yin-yang concept of opposite and complementary energies, we find extreme pain and displeasure on the one side, and extreme joy and pleasure on the other. It's not likely that we can know much about pleasure without having previously experienced displeasure—in other words, something that made us feel uncomfortable or prevented us from feeling pleasure. Only when we have known pain can we experience its opposite and feel how comfortable or peaceful we are in a given situation or with a given person. The lack of what was pleasant allows us to know, by contrast, how much we wish to have that which made us feel well. For example, we walk every day without ever realizing that we do, or how we do it, until a pebble slides itself into our shoe or we hurt our foot. If our human existence was like that of the rest of the animals on the planet, flowing naturally between the energy opposites of that which feels comfortable or "good" and that which feels uncomfortable or "bad," we would live some time in the "pain" area and some time in the "joy" area, while the rest of the time we'd go through all the intermediate points that make up the different gradations between pain and joy.

Things aren't like that, however, for us. We, civilized human beings, have forgotten how to allow the natural flow of life. Our rational mind is programmed to control or resist this natural cycle through a tangle of beliefs and of mental and emotional habits that make up an artificial energy identity. Theorists have called this aspect of our selves "ego." This ego only wants and accepts joy, while avoiding and rejecting pain. Through this cultural conditioning, pain is no longer an energy experience and comes to be associated with fear, complaint, shame, guilt, frustration, anger, and many other negative feelings. It's interesting to note that when circumstances are favorable to artificial identity (that is, when everything happens as we wish or as we are programmed to have it happen), we feel intensely happy and believe that this state should be permanent. Energetically speaking, we are totally "given over" and our pendulum shifts to the utmost joy. But when there is an experience that occurs somewhere between pain and joy, we ask ourselves what is wrong. How is it possible that there has been so much pain in my life? How is it possible that there is so much pain in the world?

The pendulum can't stay all the time in the area of joy or happiness. This is simply because things are not designed like that in the universe. It's only natural that it shifts to the center at some point, and also then to extreme pain and back to pleasure. Our existence, as well as that of everything created, is spent in a continuum going from joy to pain, but it's precisely this that our artificial identity isn't willing to accept. It rejects this part of the story and struggles to death against it. This is so because our rational mind has been programmed to avoid pain and resorts through every conceivable strategy to resist the natural movement of the pendulum. This resistance only delays the course of the oscillation, which sometimes, on its way to extreme pain, remains fixed at the pain side during a longer time than necessary—which is precisely what we are trying to avoid. Thus, the resonance of what we have been so used to feeling—suffering—is actually a direct result of the resistance to pain, which is then perpetuated within us. The pendulum needs to complete its cycle before going back to the center. The longer we resist its natural flow, the longer we will remain on the side that "feels bad." This is why suffering is more familiar to us than joy. Unconsciously, we exhaust good feelings very quickly, while we resist unendingly the unpleasant ones.

The resonance of perpetuated suffering or pain will go on until we finally let ourselves experience it, embracing it just as it is. This state of affairs does not mean that we are going to like what will then happen or agree with it. This step is the consequence of a process of taking responsibility for one's own life and accepting what it demands of us. For many people, that acceptance takes place when the artificial identity we call self-image is weakened, and gets tired of resisting reality and fighting against it. In other cases, acceptance emerges as a consequence of making friends with life and becoming aware that the pendulum's oscillation is a natural process. Finally, we come to the realization that we don't always want to live on the positive side any longer, because we have come to know that this delusion produces even more suffering. We understand that the oscillation is a natural part of our existence as human beings, and the more we accept it, the quicker the pendulum moves. At the same time, the more imperceptible the oscillation becomes. We now are no longer interested in either extreme. We recognize that the central point of the pendulum is the only one that remains firmly in its place, and consequently is the point of power.

The center of the pendulum is the witness within us, that which records the experience and "is aware." It isn't male or female. It isn't young or old. It's just the place "to be aware."

And that witness is aware with all particles constituting our being and our body-mind system. It permeates everything we call "good" or "pleasant," as well as that which we call "bad" or "unpleasant."

All that exists, if it exists, possesses that permeating "presence." If it's part of the universe, it's part of "the energy broth that creates everything and is everything."

The ego's fight against "what is" is a lost battle, so that sooner or later acceptance and giving over is inevitable. It's only a matter of time. Years? Lives? Of course, one can fight countless battles in a long, worrisome, and costly war. It all depends on the time one is willing to spend at the front and on the vital power one is willing to pay as a price.

Real versus Imaginary Pain: How We Create Suffering

Everyone has experienced physical or emotional pain at some time. There are, however, two different kinds of pain, which come from quite diverse "places." One of them is called real pain, and the other, imaginary pain, or more commonly called suffering.

Suffering is always created by our unconscious resistance to real pain, but real pain does not demand suffering. When we speak of pain, we're referring to a very comprehensive type of pain, defined as a contraction of energy.

We can experience pain in different levels: physically or emotionally. In fact, when we hear the word "pain," we often think of acute physical or emotional manifestations. Pain can also be described as discomfort, tension, stress, or be perceived as something untimely or "out of place." Pain is anything that prevents us from feeling well with ourselves or anything that doesn't feel well within ourselves.

Real Pain

We feel real pain, for instance, when we hurt our foot. The wound signals are immediately detected by minute receptors in the nerve endings of the affected organ or part of the body. Those signals are transmitted through the nerve endings to the spinal cord and instantly reach the brain to be decoded and classified. The pain sensation is immediately triggered and sent back to the foot in order to awaken the immediate consciousness of danger, and later on to facilitate healing by immobilizing the wounded area. When there's real pain, the sensation is the response of the brain to electrochemical (or neural-hormonal) changes in the wounded area. On the emotional or psychic level, we suffer real pain when we lose someone (or even an animal) we loved or were very close to. The bonds and connections we had with that person or animal, though unseen by human eyes, were very real. This kind of loss can be profoundly painful, as if a part of us had been torn off.

In CMR sessions, people describe those energy injuries in many ways. Personally, when my wife Adriana died, I felt for many weeks as if a cannonball had gone through my stomach leaving a huge hole. That entire area of my body became very weak, I walked with a stoop and needed to sit down now and then in order to breathe deeply and rest. Other people tell me they feel as if they lost a limb or as if they had a hole or crevice through which their strength was drained. When there's real pain, it's most important to acknowledge it, to give it a place, and to feel it completely. Pain isn't a nice thing and we shouldn't expect it to be. By giving it a place and feeling it, we let it move, circulate, and be transformed. The conditioned response of denying and resisting pain only makes it worse and we end up storing it in our body for some later moment. Ignoring the pain or distracting one's attention from it does nothing but perpetuate it. Quite often in a CMR session, someone releases the pain caused by the loss of a loved one, sometimes many decades ago. Time seems to have stopped at that moment, and the natural flow of the life force remains stagnated there, where pain is still intact, waiting to be felt. Our body knows. If you let it operate, it's going to find the right posture, sounds, and related emotions for pain to circulate. The sooner we go through this process, the briefer the pain period.

Imaginary Pain

Then we have what is called imaginary pain. Unfortunately, most pain suffered by human beings is of this kind. Imaginary pain originates in the mind. When I say "mind," I mean that part of ourselves that rationalizes, comments, and interprets all that happens based on a given system of beliefs. In this way, the mind decides whether what it perceives is "good" or "bad."

Let's suppose a young woman announces to her mother, "Mom, I'm going to marry Peter." To some mothers, this could be a motive for happiness, while to others it could be just the opposite. If the mother, based on her own past experiences, believes that marriage is not a good thing, the announcement may cause her a heart attack, a deep depression, or a storm of rage or panic. This is simply because in her innermost being her belief system "tells her the story" of how unhappy her daughter will be in her marriage, or how miserable she herself will feel when she sees her daughter suffer. When imaginary pain is triggered, it hurts because our mind has decreed an inner emergency state based on beliefs and decisions that have been elaborated during past painful experiences. Imaginary pain originates in the mind and is immediately transferred to the body, causing every sort of problem, because it often remains stagnated, without being either explored or processed. Then, each time something triggers that memory, which is kept in what I call the submerged portion of the "iceberg" that we are—in other words, in the subconscious—we'll think and feel as we thought and felt when we had the original pain, this time without knowing why or understanding what is happening.

Since we are culturally trained to reject pain and not feel it, the body keeps that pain guarded for a later moment. And it becomes a vicious circle, endlessly hurting. Whenever there is imaginary pain, there is a mind that generates it and a physical and emotional body triggering sensations and feelings that want to move. The mental becomes physical, confusing, and distorting, resisting what was real in the past and what is real in the present. Reeducating our mind and reprogramming the toxic thoughts, beliefs, and unconscious presumptions can be done, and what we call suffering will go away with them.

Chronic Pain

Imaginary pain generates suffering and also makes it last longer. The more imaginary pain there is within us, the more suffering we'll have. Energy contractions created by imaginary pain alter our organic, nervous, and structural functioning. A chronic pain may be the result of layers upon layers of imaginary pain, but it may also be the result of an old illness or accident. In the latter case, the chronic pain is the combination of:

> the original pain (a wound, an injury, a tumor, an organic dysfunction)
> + the resistance to feel it ("this shouldn't happen," "it's too much for me")
> + the imaginary pain (the fear to be disabled, the fear of the future, the fear of death, etc.).

If we asked a person with a chronic pain what score, from zero to ten—where zero represents well-being and ten a very intense, unbearable pain—she would ascribe to her pain, and she chooses eight, we'd know that part of that pain is real and part of it imaginary.

Now, pain can change and diminish in case the person stops resisting it and believing the stories her mind is telling her. Very likely then, the original real pain will change and healing will naturally occur. This is what happens in most cases I've treated through CMR. When there is chronic pain, there is also a history and a self-image created by having suffered for some time. When we are used to being ill or aching, we think that we "possess" the illness. (Quite often, we hear people saying "my arthritis" or "my tumor.") Releasing these stagnated energy charges, that hypothetical number eight could be lowered down to much more manageable levels, to one or even to zero. However, there are exceptions, as always, and facts can be different. I've seen many people heal their chronic pain by simply canceling out the system of beliefs that sustained them. (See the examples mentioned in Chapters 9 and 10.) Others have to go beyond the process of canceling out beliefs. They have to permit themselves to feel the pain created by those beliefs and to cancel out the resulting self-image. This implies radical changes in perception, habits, and behaviors. Still others have to go even deeper, crudely and wholly feeling and reliving the original pain, sometimes reaching to prenatal experiences and even to generational resonances, or to the simple and pure pain common to all humans.

When somebody comes to consult us, we never know what is going to happen. Why some people can solve their problem with only retrieving a childhood wound, while others must come in touch with ancestral resonances dating back many generations, is not known. Regardless of where those resonances come from, in our therapeutic work we always regard them as present energy.

It's Wise to Avoid Pain; It Isn't Wise to Resist It

Every human being is designed to instinctively avoid pain. To keep away from painful situations is instinctive wisdom. To avoid situations in which we could be hurt is to make use of the natural abilities we have by the mere fact of having been born. You wouldn't put your hand on the burner if you knew it was too hot and could harm you! Nevertheless, when pain is already manifested, it's too late to avoid it. We must go out to meet it and, as Rumi says, tell it to come in. This is the key to transforming pain, to healing quickly, and to living a life free of suffering.

Anyone can see the difference between civilized adults, on the one hand, and animals and little children, on the other, in the way they relate to pain. When a small child is sad, she cries. When she's angry, she screams. When she's afraid, she trembles. In this way, children honor what they feel. When children feel pain: they allow themselves to have the sensation or feeling (because they haven't learned to do the opposite yet); they allow their bodies to naturally process "the unpleasant" (crying, screaming, or shaking); they exaggerate, intensifying what they feel until it's over; and finally they relax. Some minutes later, they behave as if nothing happened and go back to play.

In civilized adults this process is remarkably different. They are experts in emotional dishonesty and in pretending that they don't feel what they feel. When they are sad, they say to themselves and to the others, "Nothing happened." When they are angry, they say to themselves and to others, "Everything is all right." When they are afraid, they behave as if everything is under control. However, those same people act differently when they have pleasant and socially accepted sensations and feelings that, furthermore, will bring them rewards if they communicate them. The only acceptable and respectable thing to do is to express those happy sentiments that can be related to the sunny side of life. In that case, a person will experience, express, and exhaust those feelings quickly, and will soon want and need more.

When we describe a feeling as negative we're resisting its existence. When we deny something we feel and judge ourselves for feeling it, we are denying a true part of ourselves. It is very possible that in our childhood at one time we may have felt furious at one of our parents. If we had felt that our home was a safe place for the expression of this emotion, we would have communicated our feelings instantly and without hesitation. If that wasn't the case, we probably masked our feelings according to what we thought was expected from us. Perhaps we repressed that fury and replaced it with guilty and shameful feelings, while we said to ourselves, "What kind of son am I that feels this way toward his mother?" It's also likely that we resorted to another very common strategy, that of suppressing the emotion by covering it with fear. "If I tell her what I feel, she's going to kill me," or in a more sublimated version, "She's going to leave me," or simply, "She won't love me anymore." We have grown up and have been educated to replace what we feel with something more consistent with our artificial identity and with the imaginary scenarios about "how things should be in our family" (or "in this couple" or "in this society").

We have probably lived much of our life resisting what happened to us in one or several of the following ways:

ACTION	INNER DIALOG
Denial	"Everything is all right, there's no problem."
Judgment	"This shouldn't happen."
Avoidance	"What can I do to distract my attention from it?"
Medication	"I'll take a tranquilizer."
Complaint	"Why does this always happen to me?"
Analysis	"What does all this mean?"
Pray	"Please, my God, help me here!"
Visualization	"I imagine that I am feeling good …"
Blame	"It's my fault [or his fault or her fault] …"
Predicting	"If this is happening now, that is going to happen then."

EXERCISE

Take a piece of paper and a pencil, and answer the following questions:

- Which of these forms of resistance and denial have you resorted to in your life?
- Which of them are you still using?
- Write down any other form of resistance to pain that isn't on the list. Pay attention to your body and what you feel while doing this.

If we resist "what is" and our current feelings, we won't be able to digest the experience. This will translate into an extremely unpleasant, sometimes unbearable, sensation. In energy terms, unpleasant or disagreeable emotions are stored and originate contractions that form what we call the pain body. The pain body is the accumulation of every uncomfortable sensorial experience or unpleasant emotion that was not acknowledged or permitted to be felt when it was occurring. These feelings were always resisted and, as a consequence, never processed.

The pain body is the sum of all the negative and painful experiences we've had, of all physical and emotional trauma, of all feelings of fear, shame, guilt, anger, and sadness we didn't permit ourselves to feel. It's also formed by the contractions created in us by what I call "prophetic mind," that part of our rational mind that tends to anticipate the future and generates several kinds of anxiety, fear, anger, and sadness out of "what could happen next." We have been—and are being—programmed to perceive life in a way that causes us to suffer. This is the result of both ignorance and imitation. Most human suffering is imaginary, and as such unnecessary.

Resisting Is Suffering

We often dislike what is happening to us and live in a state of nearly constant dissatisfaction. We are rarely happy with our lives. Besides, our "civilized programming" gives rise to the collective belief that we're never sufficiently adequate or complete. This is the basic belief underlying progress, and it may have a beneficial side—but at a very high emotional cost. "I don't like this way of living," "I'm not ready," "It's too much for me," "This shouldn't happen now"—these thoughts come to our mind when we can't acknowledge the simple truth that everything in the universe is flowing, and that our vital force must flow with life in the same way that a river must flow to the ocean. In denying anything that might happen, we're fighting against the universe and the whole of creation. It must be understood that this is a lost fight from the very beginning, because the plans imbuing the universe—and everything that was created in it—are very powerful. When we think in terms of "it should be" or "it shouldn't be," we ignore the fact that everything happens for a reason, and though we may not know the reason, it's supported by the creative force of all that exists.

When our rational mind produces thoughts about our life circumstances that come from resistance and denial, the vital force flowing naturally within us comes to a standstill, stagnates, and accumulates. This accumulation process gives origin to an excess of energy called "negative emotional charge" and to physical or emotional suffering. Imagine a river that flows naturally until, at a certain point, its waters are blocked by a dam. The result will be a large volume of stagnated water. There will be an excess of water upriver while there will be a lack of it downriver. The enormous pressure caused by the dam, together with the resulting ecological imbalance, will affect not only the river but everything around it. The same happens when we "dam" a sensation or a feeling: the vital force remains trapped in our body just as the river water is blocked by the dam and generates the pain body. It gives rise to a negative energy resonance affecting our physical, emotional, and spiritual well-being.

Chinese medicine has two golden rules that help us understand in what way pain is created. The first of them is "when the vital force (chi) is stagnated, illnesses appear." The second is "when there is pain, there is an excess of accumulated energy (chi)." The excess of energy trapped in the circuits of the body-mind system generates at all levels what is known in this kind of medicine as a yin/yang energy imbalance. On one side, there is an excess of energy, while on the other there is not enough. Together, yin and yang represent the dynamic, creative, and eternal movement of the universe, and are also present in us, since we are part of the universe. If we resist accepting either of them in us, or deny their existence, our vital force will become stagnated as unhealthy energy. We will be unconnected with life and with our own being, and suffering will remain our most faithful companion.

Thus, to deny or resist what life gives us is equivalent to damming the current of the river with solid rock. "You can't swim against the tide." This refrain was coined after centuries of pain experiences. Isn't it clear enough? If we change our response, if we accept that "it's happening to me now and, therefore, exists," we allow the stagnated vital force to flow again and eventually to transform itself. We can fight against our life force for as long as we wish, we can deny it and resist it till death, but we can also try to make an alliance with it to do such work together as must be done. We can ignore pain as long as we wish, but if we give it a place and listen to it, the door of a crucial transformation process will open before us. Once we commit ourselves to our life and wholly embrace it, the miracle of ease will visit us.

CHAPTER 4

Suffering-Addiction: the Compulsion to Suffer

"Let us not forget this: spiritual consciousness and human thought are quite different things. Thought can begin the search but cannot discover what is real. The human mind can unfurl the sails and start the journey, but then it must stand aside and rest, leaving it to the winds of Truth to carry us to our destination."
—Vernon Howard

Pain Happens, While Suffering Is Optional

"That which resists, persists," says a very old dictum borrowed from Eastern spiritual teachings. Though in some circles it has become a cliché, there is great wisdom in it. Pain can come into our lives in many ways. To resist it is, above all, to deny that it already is with us and to go on blindly fighting against what happens. But to struggle with pain is to struggle with reality, and, according to our experience, to struggle with reality is almost always a bad deal.

Pain is part of human life as much as pleasure and joy. The best we can do to avoid suffering is to allow things to happen and to embrace our

life. But to allow things to happen doesn't mean to like them or to agree
with them. Neither does it mean that we shouldn't try to do something
to change them. To honor our life and embrace it definitively, there
is no need to like everything that happens to us. Embracing, loving,
and honoring our life only demands being present and feeling with
our conscious awareness whatever we feel at any given moment. To be
present does not mean to stop the mind, but to observe it and, from
that place of contemplation and presence, to embrace our life such as
it is and become not its enemy but its ally.

Life is being constantly created and supported by the whole
universe. It couldn't be otherwise. The ideas we have about how our life
should be come from that artificial identity we call self-image, which
uses our mind to generate one new fantasy after the other, which are
the obstacles to embracing what is really going on. To ally oneself with
the universe of which we are undeniably a part, and to flow in the
incessant creation of that which we call "our life," constitutes a deep
and powerfully wise act. When our energy center of gravity is aligned
with the life flow, we can sense love, power, and freedom. Then we
are like a drop of water celebrating being part of the ocean. We can
live at high speed, leaping from one experience to another. So what
would happen if instead of running like the hamster within a giant
self-fantasized wheel, we stopped to live thoroughly, honoring each
experience and event as it occurs? What if, instead of spending our
energy getting anxious trying to carry out our grand plans, predictions,
and ideas, we admitted that those plans and ideas are, in fact, part of
the same universe that recreates itself through us? If we accepted this
reality, we would feel at ease, because we would realize that what must
be will be, and what must be done will be done, through us.

By virtue of the process of individual programming and conditioning
along many generations, we have been taught to believe that if we
don't make something happen, it won't happen. I think this is the same
as watering a garden when it is already raining. An inner attitude of

flowing with life demands great creative power. To make an alliance with the movement of the universe as it is manifested in what we call our life is to let powerful change occur, changes that are already there, waiting to be allowed to occur, in agreement with some other plan that may not be conceived of by our conditioned mind. The discussion of this subject is necessary because it enables us to detect and cancel out those areas of our life in which suffering prevails. Eckhart Tolle advises what we should do when trouble or nuisance affects our life. He says that when we are at peace with ourselves, flowing with life, we have always three nonsuffering options; however, most often we choose a fourth, which is, precisely, suffering. My version of these options are:

1. *To change what I don't like, or to ask for what I want, to be ready to receive a "no" answer, and to negotiate as needed.* This means to use every possible means to change the situation. If I'm cold, I put on some clothes or look for shelter; if I'm hungry, I eat; if I've no food, I ask or search for it; if I'm ill, I try to heal myself; etc. If I have trouble in a relationship with somebody, I resort to conscious communication, speaking honestly, expressing how I feel and what my needs are. I make all my requests knowing that the answer to everything I ask for may be "no" but also "yes." I implement every needed change, convinced that if changes are possible, it means that the universe agrees with them, or, in other words, that the universe makes changes through me. Now, even if doing every possible thing I can't change the situation, there are two more options available without losing peace of mind.

2. *To accept wholly and thoroughly what is happening without blaming anybody or complaining about anything, while at peace with myself.* This doesn't mean to give up or surrender, which would imply generating emotional contractions full of sadness, resentment, fear, or guilt. When we accept life and are allied with it, we find ways to enjoy it such as it is. Accepting after trying every possible change—or even while we are trying—gives us a lot of energy and makes us much more creative. By

virtue of the law of attraction, we thus attract into our life energies similar to ours. In the cases of chronic or terminal illnesses, incurable physical disabilities, tragedies, accidents, or the death of a loved one, this attitude may provide a lot of inner peace and strength. Besides, it increases the ability of our body to heal itself, because it is not spending its vital force in imaginary pain. There are countless examples of people who were able to improve their quality of life in a surprising way just by finding their inner peace and making an alliance with life instead of resisting it. But if I can change nothing and it's impossible for me to accept, there is still one more option to exercise without losing peace.

3. To remove myself from the situation is the third available option without losing my inner peace. Let's give an example. Suppose I've come to realize that one of the most relevant needs in my life is to be at peace and enjoy it, but my work demands that I remain shut up inside an office all day long, surrounded by a tense and noisy working environment, where people quarrel all the time. Then—

I resort to my first option and try to change the situation. I talk about it with my boss, ask for a transfer to another department, etc. Even so, if nothing changes, I try to accept the situation such as it is. However, I can't. At the end of the day I'm exhausted, in bad temper, and my mind incessantly judges and complains. In other words, I suffer. In that case, I set in motion the third option: I leave the situation behind. I look for another way of earning a living that is more consistent with my principles, priorities, and life values.

What is important is to be clear about not negotiating our inner peace at any cost. It's easier said than done, I know. The main obstacle I've found in myself and in other people is that we're culturally programmed to be victims, to complain and suffer—and this is the fourth option we nearly always choose. We saw this option exercised while we grew up and continue to see it everywhere. We have seen our family, teachers, and many other people suffering, not enjoying their lives, and became convinced that it was natural and normal. "Life is suffering," they say, and we agree, we believe it, and we turn it into truth. It can only be natural and normal inasmuch as we are unaware of whom and what we really are. When we believe that we are what we aren't, we live lying to ourselves. And the natural consequence of lying to oneself is suffering.

When we ignore that we can choose between the options and continuously pick the same option—to be a victim—then it's almost impossible to be at peace with ourselves. In other words, we inadvertently choose to complain, to be anxious or worried. We choose to accumulate resentment, to accuse and blame others, to lie and hide, and to use many other strategies in order not to take responsibility for our lives.

EXERCISE

Take a piece of paper and a pencil. Think about your life and try to detect the areas in which there is suffering. Answer questions 1 through 7, keeping in mind that your aim is to live at peace and to enjoy life.

1. Is there anything I can do to change this situation? Yes No
2. I can change ....
   ....
   ....
3. Am I willing to change? Yes No
4. Can I accept this situation such as it is? Yes No
5. Am I willing to accept it? Yes No
6. Can I remove myself from it? Yes No
7. Am I willing to remove myself from it? Yes No

A suggestion: Start with something easy, such as "I don't like that my desk is always a mess," or "I know I've got a cavity but I won't go to the dentist." Then choose something much more complicated, such as "I don't like how my legs look," or "I don't like my daughter's boyfriend."

The Victim Virus: the Suffering-Addiction

To play the role of victim is part of a very old cultural model, as old as our civilization. We find this pattern in all of human history. Today, it's present in the books we read, in the TV programs we watch, in the daily news, in religions, in national and international politics, in schools, in couples, in the family, in friendships, and so on and so forth. We're so used to this role that it has become an addiction. In fact, this addiction is a socially accepted one in which much physical, mental, and emotional misery is perpetuated. To be a victim is a cultural game that has already taken, and continues to take, many casualties among us. The person who plays the role of victim is suffering for different reasons and causes. She may suffer because of unfulfilled basic needs, physical ailments or illnesses, lack of energy, fatigue, helplessness, despair, indifference, unachieved recognition, confusion, betrayal, physical, emotional, or sexual abuse, or because she has been manipulated, exploited, oppressed, abandoned, persecuted, among other things.

The resonance that is activated when we feel like a victim generates unconscious thoughts and behaviors, and we find ourselves silently or outwardly complaining, blaming ourselves or others, or life, or God. This chronic complaining state creates inner contractions that prevent essential energies from flowing as they should, and drain our vital force. This is extremely debilitating. According to the law of attraction and its principles, when we send out the resonance of "the victim," we attract to us persons and situations that will make us suffer. Furthermore, we can't make the most of the experience we're living and will repeat them endlessly in various ways. The victim "virus" leads us to perceive ourselves as an entity separated from the whole, having constantly to defend or attack. This "virus" also gives rise to a chronic fear resonance and sets forth a vicious cycle: the more afraid I am, the more separated I feel; the more separated I feel, the more alone I am; the more alone I am, the more must I protect myself from what others may do to me, or from what can happen to me; the more I must protect and defend myself, the more I blame; the more I blame and accuse the other, the more separated I feel; and the more separated I feel, the more afraid I am. In this vicious cycle, the root cause of human suffering returns to its beginnings.

How to Detect When One Is Playing the Role of Victim

When playing the role of victim:

We react unconsciously to everything.

Our mind constantly creates situations full of anxiety or worry.

We think, interpret, and analyze (inwardly or outwardly).

We deny what we feel ("Everything is all right," "There's no problem," etc.).

We suppress our emotions (with rigidity, contractions, tensions, and illnesses).

We tend to engage in dramatic situations and with dramatic persons.

We permanently speak about what "should" and "shouldn't" be done.

We complain about ourselves and others.

We inwardly or outwardly judge, criticize, accuse, and blame anyone.

We repeat past situations again and again in our mind.

We find it very difficult to forgive, and keep very old resentments.

We want to take revenge and "collect debts."

We resort to our painful past when having to act or make decisions in the present.

We are afraid of the future and of what it may have in store for us.

We rehearse again and again what we shall do or say.

We aren't aware of the present and ignore it completely.

Now, write down which of these traits are true in your case.

The Model of Self-Responsibility

The model of self-responsibility is the opposite of the role of victim; it implies honoring life and is connected with the light body.

The way to achieve it is by:

Acknowledging what I feel: "I'm scared, angry, sad, excited, enthused, attracted by ..."

Localizing the feelings: realizing in what part of the body is exactly localized the sensation.

Permitting the feelings: moving oneself, shaking oneself, stretching, emitting sounds, etc.

Intensifying the feelings: amplifying to the greatest possible degree what one feels.

Breathing into the feelings.

When I take responsibility for my life, I become the protagonist; an active participant in it. Then, I can be proactive in making the changes I want, in accepting what is or in removing myself from the uncomfortable situation.

CHAPTER 5
The Pain Body

"There are two levels of pain: the pain you create now, and the pain of the past that is still alive in your mind and your body. Of course, this includes the pain with which you have been born. The accumulated pain is a negative energy occupying your mind and your body. If you regard it as an invisible entity in its own right, you'll be approaching the truth. It is the pain body."
—Eckhart Tolle, *The Power of Now*

Recovery of Lost Parts

We have said that if there's something that all human beings—from every culture and time—agree upon, it is the existence of pain, whether physical, emotional, or spiritual. To live life is, among many other experiences, to discover pain and carry it on one's back, often hidden in a backpack or rucksack. While we walk along, we continue to take up stones and throw them into it, in the hope that some day we will be able to take all of them out and select them. However, usually we must cope with the rucksack's content earlier than we had expected. In primitive cultures, the healer and the sorcerer were one and the same person: the shaman. He was able to treat pain as an entity in its own right, for which he first acknowledged its existence and then exorcized or expelled it. Our ancestors released themselves of their sins through the ritual of finding a scapegoat. Many historical or contemporary religious rituals have had their origin in this deep human need of releasing, expelling, and discharging pain or fear.

In our culture, so permeated by technology and mostly agnostic, these practices, as well as ritual prayers and dances and all celebrations having to do with life and death cycles, have become obsolete and discredited. Where can we find a spiritual way that is not ruled by rigid and exclusionary dogmas? To what temple of knowledge can we resort in our need to find a course for that vital function of transforming energy, such as many peoples have done for centuries on end? If some reliable person could let us know where to search for this and what to do, the whole enterprise would be quite exciting. Many of us have already picked enough stones along the way to keep in our rucksacks, so that from now on we might want to begin throwing them out so as to walk less burdened, to stop looking down, to walk with our head held high, and to be open to innocent admiration and the embrace of the light body. Now, that would be very good news for all of us. We would then have no secrets from our own body. We would know all roads and have all the answers. That incredibly wise body has been waiting while our mind has been busy doing other things, establishing its own comprehensive agenda. As a faithful friend of ours since our childhood, it actually contains many sad and happy moments, most of which we have chosen to forget, and it knows what we need. Perhaps the moment has come for us to listen to what it has to tell us.

When we decide to listen, as soon as we begin our investigation we'll find out that our holistic being is like a big mansion with dozens of empty, unused rooms, while we live withdrawn and constrained into a small area of it. We do not even know what there is in the rest of that big house. We have lived our existence only in the kitchen; there we have made our food, slept, and even entertained our guests, while beyond the kitchen there are a lot of large and sumptuous rooms with their doors shut, full of spiderwebs because nobody has inhabited or visited them for decades. So we take a flashlight and, under its faint, hesitant light, we begin to go all over the house and discover incredible places, some of them quite untidy, some full of insects and pests, the existence of which we completely ignored. We begin to feel a tingling sensation, a sort of eagerness, because we suspect that all those places can be transformed and used—cleaned up, decorated, inhabited. Then before our eyes all the work we have put off for some time will appear, all the things that were stopped at some point, like in a fairy tale in which the characters were under a spell and slept a long time, each in their place, until years later they woke up and went on living. So something shifts and everything is wired again.

When this process begins, it is good to focus on one "place," one area, and to record—perhaps by writing it down—the work that one is doing there. The best thing to do is to keep a diary or notebook in which to make notes and comments that no one else can read. There you can write things like, "I discovered the following connections related to my mother (my father, my aunt, etc.). Later I will see where they lead. For the time being, I'll finish what I've already begun." Some studies have demonstrated that in calm or quiet states of mind, the frontal lobes of our brain are naturally activated. Curiously enough, this is the area of our brain where creativity and the ability to make new innovative decisions are lodged. There are people who use that area a lot because their type of work or profession demands them to anticipate results—whether their task is to paint a picture, to redesign a room, or to organize a public event. In stressful states, the bloodstream abandons the frontal area of the brain and concentrates in the back part of it, where survival mechanisms learned a long time ago are aroused. That back part is where memory and all records of past experiences, including our ancestral and primitive past, are kept. The more we explore our brain, the further we reach backward into the history of our origins.

Our modern, stressful mode of living makes us live largely through the rear part of our brain, leaving the front area vacant during a vast portion of our life. Returning to the metaphor of the empty mansion, we find ourselves living in the kitchen, constantly recycling thoughts and events, cooking new plates with the leftovers from yesterday. Thus cooked, no meal has the same taste or smells like a new one—like new ideas, possibilities, projects—that, prepared with well-chosen ingredients, can only come from the frontal area of the brain when it is properly activated. In this transformation process, there often emerges descriptions and stories related to the creative fire. At all times and cultures, saints and mystics have regarded fire as a purifying element, have lived through darkness and death on one plane, and through some sort of rebirthing on another. These people have had access to those experiences putting aside their ego in a meditative state or a prayer.

How the Pain Body Is Created

The human body can be affected by layers of stagnated energy called "negative emotional charge." Eckhart Tolle has called these strata of accumulated energy the pain body. Our body cells, which keep in them the physical and emotional pain or trauma of the past, operate according to a survival pattern that is only real for the person who believes in it. Any unresolved trauma gives rise to stagnation in some part of the energy field and prevents the natural flow of vital force through the physical body. Frequently, it manifests itself in the organs, muscles, or joints that are associated with the trauma. The negative emotional charge of stagnated energy areas literally splits the human energy field in "watertight compartments" with no possible communication among them. When we prevent the conscious transformation of the trauma, we favor the accumulation of further layers of negative emotional charge, making the situation even more difficult and complex.

Let's take an example: You fall down in the street and you hurt one ankle. Perhaps you get furious with yourself for not having paid enough attention when walking, and blame yourself, saying things like, "You're stupid, you never pay attention," or "You're always late," or "You always do the same thing, you deserve it for being such an idiot." Then you don't feel only the physical pain—which is real—but have added to it anger, fear, judgment, and self-condemnation—which are imaginary. This mechanism can repeat itself endlessly. In his book *You Can Heal Now*, acupuncturist Tapas Fleming writes, "When the moment a trauma (whether physical, emotional, or spiritual) occurs we feel that life is unbearable and say NO to anything that might be happening to us." Perhaps you don't recognize this situation as your own, but there are several variants in the way of expressing it: "This can't be happening to me," "Why has it happened precisely to me?" "This is too much for me to bear," and "If this happens, I won't be able to survive it."

These expressions mean that we inwardly affirm, "I'll take care of this later; for the time being, I'll leave it aside. I'll face it when I'm able to, provided it doesn't threaten my life." But we go on putting it off, leaving aside that which we don't want to confront now, and thus the energy and imbalance of the undigested, unresolved trauma remains with us. We can distance ourselves from the fact in space and time, but the experience will continue to be present in our energy field.

Besides putting things off, we are used to denying them. For instance, "Between Mom and me everything is OK, we have no problems," or "That was silly, childish behavior." But the longer we try to keep the negative emotional charge secluded in what we call the past, the more intensely we connect with it and the more unresolved business keeps emerging, imposing even more limitations on our lives. Besides, unprocessed trauma suffocates and diminishes the positive emotional charge, leading to an important dysfunction in the body-mind system. The negative emotional charge (or pain body) is so disproportionate in regards to the positive one, that natural bodily functions are deeply affected. Think of the amount of vital force needed to keep the negative emotional charge stored in cells for such a long time. Now try to imagine how we would feel if we could release that negative charge and give way to a transformation. Indeed, that operation is possible through the use of techniques that, while releasing the stagnated vital force, don't erase memory. Cells are thus provided a natural and free energy that they can use for their growth and self-healing.

The pain body is an inner energy field created by genetic conditioning, the belief system in which we have been raised, and the negative decisions we made in the past. Sometimes, the stimuli triggering the pain body seem trivial to other people, who can't understand our exaggerated and dramatic responses. The fact that we are seemingly misunderstood generates even more negative perceptions and thoughts in us, attracting to us further unpleasant experiences. The resonance of the pain body is dominant and ever present in our culture: in the books we read, the films, TV series, and soap operas we watch, etc. It would seem that everyone wants more pain body in every place and in whatever expression. The pain body manifests itself every day in stress, anxiety, anger, jealousy, oppression, resentment, fear, guilt, shame, and many other negative forms.

When we go through any inner tension, we usually make unconscious decisions based on such ideas as "I'm not good enough" or "I won't be able to do it." These decisions are tinted with a negative perception of ourselves and, if we believe in it, it leaves its imprint in our energy field and conducts our life. For the most part, those imprints have been stamped on us during our childhood—a crucial time in our development as human beings—or even might have been absorbed from our mother's energy field during intrauterine life. Some others may have been genetically inherited, in the same way we inherit a talent for music or sports.

We have a resistance to working consciously with the pain body, either because we ignore its existence or because we don't know how to do it. The pain body can be released only when we transform the negative emotional charge that is stagnated in our system. The practice of the techniques suggested in this book may let us visit (perhaps for the first time in our life) our energy field with an increased awareness of our own mind and of our physical and emotional reality.

Some Particular Traits of the Pain Body

- The pain body isn't a problem of some individuals only, but is a trait common to all humans.
- The pain body is the pain each human being inherits and shares with others.
- Nations and societies also have their own collective pain body, shared by all their members.
- The pain body is a pain remnant.
- It's the combined result of the resistance to and denial of something we experienced.
- It's recognized when some insignificant event triggers a disproportionate response.
- It's also recognized in your reaction when something goes wrong or when someone says something you find annoying.
- The pain body emerges when the vital force can't flow freely. Then, pressure accumulates and pain appears.
- When the pain body emerges, the feeling of unhappiness and emptiness increases up to an unbearable level.
- If we attempt to flee or to fight it, the pain grows.
- Symptoms of the pain body are different in each person. It may be perceived as a turbulence, a constraint, a "rock" in the solar plexus, a "ball" in the throat, a sensation of heaviness or heat, or a feeling of dizziness, terror, or intense pressure.
- The pain body may be submissive or aggressive.
- The pain body may be passive or active. There are those that are always active, as happens with people who suffer addictions, depression, chronic irritability, or physical pain.
- The vital force is often trapped in the pain body.
- The pain body must go out to feed itself from time to time. Its feeding period varies from one person to another; it may be once a day, once a week, or once a month.

- Once fed, the pain body gains control over our mind and gives rise to destructive, negative thoughts.
- The pain body is intensely addictive; once it has taken control over the person's mind—and, consequently, her responses—that person doesn't want to be at peace anymore, but "needs" to go on suffering.
- The pain body needs the others´ responses and feeds on them. If the individual is alone, it reviews again what happened or imagines what is going to happen, in order to create uneasiness and inner tension.
- When someone's pain body is ready to emerge, it attempts to provoke reactions in the pain body of his nearest and dearest.

- The pain body likes drama. Unfortunately, most relationships are full of drama, and when a dramatic situation occurs, the mind already aligned with the pain body will find any excuse to add some of its usual tricks to a heated argument or a tense confrontation.
- To acknowledge our pain body is the beginning of a healing and transformation process. As the trapped energy is released, the individual's health, vitality, and creativity increase.

- When we accept and observe the pain body, we cut its links with the mind and control it. Then, the only residue it leaves in us is an uncomfortable energy field.
- The pain body isn't our enemy. Don't fight against it or try to eliminate it.
- The stronger the pain body, the stronger the motive to transform it.
- What is called karma—that is, the unconscious repetition of past energy patterns—can be consciously dissolved when the pain body is transformed.

Being part of the human race, each of us shares a part of a collective pain and registers in her the conditioning of millions of social, cultural, genetic, and planetary influences.

What Is Not "Real" Creates Pain: How Our Thoughts Affect Our State of Being

Will you carry your garbage can to a sacred temple? Surely not. However, our culture provides us with our programming from our first breath that fills our mind with a lot of "viruses," and lies.

Emotions are our feelings in movement and our feelings are generated by the thoughts we think. Our feelings and emotions in action create attitudes and behaviors. Then, we need to explain and support those behaviors with thoughts in the form of ideas and interpretations. Those thoughts will generate more of the same feelings and emotions, feeding in us the endless cycle of repetitive patterns.

Thought – Feeling – Behavior – Inner dialogue - Thought

Modern science has discovered that there are two main processes that our cells perform. Cells reproduce and expand (harmony) or protect and contract (fear).

In his book "The Biology of Beliefs," Dr. Bruce Lipton tells us that historically medical texts have explained evolution and behavior starting with DNA dismissing the role of proteins and the environment (our life situation) in cellular health and balance. He also explains how this is insufficient and shows us, scientifically, how environmental stimulus 'triggers' intercellular proteins; and it is these proteins that enact the DNA. In this way, a cancer gene lies dormant until the environment stimulates it. He points that to fully support cellular health we can no longer ignore the role of consciousness and that includes our own thinking.

Lipton also says that our general health is not so much affected by our environment directly but our perception of it, and goes one step further by linking perception (belief) to cellular health and behavior. He further explains that cellular health, growth, and reproduction respond favorably to thoughts of love and harmony whereas the so-called negative thoughts create the opposite in us.

Feelings are created in our body by thoughts that we believe. If we believe in a lie, our cells contract and toxic energy elements accumulate within us and give rise to dysfunction and lack of vitality. Thoughts are very valuable and they may highly contribute to our life experience. The fact that we can't see, weigh, or measure them doesn't make them any less important. The rational mind—with all its thoughts and opinions—has the power to prompt powerful energy movements in us. It's a miraculous creation and deserves to be regarded as such. The mind is constantly triggering sensations and feelings in our body because our cells expand or contract following them. Our energy field is very dynamic and is changing constantly. Most often, changes begin to act upon our thoughts.

CHAPTER 6
Cells Remember

"Memories are not only stored in the brain, but also in the
psychosomatic network extending throughout the body, along the
connections between organs and even in our skin surface."
—Candace Pert

What Is Cellular Memory?: the Human Bio-Computer

I often compare the human body with a very sophisticated computer.
In this magnificent bio-computer, the brain isn't the only place where
memories are stored. I have observed that we also have a cellular
memory in which experiences that condition our life in a profound
way are recorded. Our cellular memory is a complex set of files lodged
in the human bio-computer. It contains information about our genetic
inheritance and all our individual history; it is an accurate recording of
our life imprinted on each of our cells like a logbook.

Information stored in the cell includes: the experiences of the soul,
the experiences of our ancestors, the culture in which we have been
raised, and our own experiences.

Each cell of our body has a memory, and each human being has a
unique total memory. This memory informs and permeates our being,

belongs, and is both of our body as well as of our mind and spirit. Stored in the cellular memory are all of the conscious and unconscious patterns that create behaviors that do not allow us to feel at peace with ourselves. Cellular memory affects the way we perform our daily routine tasks, as well as the way we react to stress and face our emotional challenges. If past wounds kept in our cellular memory are not healed, they may limit our freedom and cause illnesses to occur.

The human energy field keeps our memory and imprints energy information or "info-energy" on each and every cell of our physical body.

The sum of all these memories gives origin to a unique energy broth we call "self-image," composed of every physical, mental, and emotional trait, tendency, talent, or shortcoming we have had in our life.

Therefore, each of us vibrates in a unique energy frequency. We are energy beings that generate or attract our own "lives" in terms of the frequencies that resonate within us.

Some Aspects of Cellular Memory

Our existence is as unique as our fingerprints and is imprinted on each cell of our body. Our whole being is an intelligent, integrated, and individual hologram. We actually are a holistic being, not a sum of parts. Labels such as "body," "mind," and "spirit" are artificial, and their only use is to help us study and understand our existence as human beings. In the cell hologram, each point contains the complete information about the whole. The body may be healed if and only if the mind and the spirit are also healed. In other words, to achieve a transformation by means of this process, it must be approached in an integrated way.

Cell memory is imprinted by an energy field full of information called info-energy. If you expand the size of a cell until all its atoms are visible, you can verify that we are designed according to delicate masses of info-energy. Quantum physics has already discovered that the building blocks of visible matter are light and sound.

Cells are the hologram pieces that bear our identity and our name. Every human being has a unique life. As there are not two blades of grass that are exactly the same, there does not exist and won't ever exist, someone exactly like you or like me. The combination of physical, mental, emotional, and spiritual material is a unique masterpiece that cannot be duplicated. The human body is formed by cells that grow, differentiate, and multiply, carrying with them the basic information obtained at the instant they were conceived. This unique combination of info-energy is the foundational matrix of a human life until death, at which time the hologram disintegrates. Our body's cells are the building blocks of the hologram that represents a human being, which is in turn the main vehicle of the existential experience we call "my life."

The cells of our hologram carry with them all the physical, emotional, mental, and spiritual information. Our cells transport the deoxyribonucleic acid (DNA) including the genetic imprint and the complete design of our body. Also lodged in them are the impressions of our mental, emotional, and spiritual experiences. The cells keep information of all our genetic conditioning and of all our past experiences. This information is unconsciously alive in us, determining our every physical, emotional, and mental pattern. We are an energy conglomerate vibrating and resonating just like a musical note. The whole of humanity is somehow represented in each and every cell of our body. None of the positive or negative experiences we have escapes the highly conditioned design of our hologram. Our conscious life is like the tip of an iceberg, the visible portion representing only 3 to 5 percent of the whole that we actually are. The submerged portion of the iceberg is the subconscious portion of our life, the one that permeates cells with information and memory. The subconscious operates as if it were behind a veil, conditioning our way of perceiving and responding.

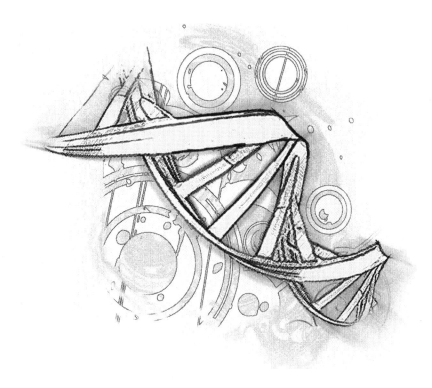

Our cells need to be part of the creative energy flow of the universe. Giving and receiving love is essential for cell growth and expansion. Our hologram has been designed to be nourished by unconditional love and grow with energy. Knowing the dynamics of cell functioning will help to understand it better. The hypothalamus is the region of the brain in charge of synthesizing proteins to adapt them to different organic functions. These special proteins—called "neuropeptides"—are released in the bloodstream each time an emotional state is triggered. Each emotional state produces many different kinds of neuropeptides, which quickly travel through the bloodstream until they find the cells with the appropriate receptors. So, our cells have a certain amount of receptors available for certain neuropeptides. For instance, we may find many receptors able to lodge neuropeptides generated by the sadness or frustration of a person who is permanently depressed. On the other hand, that same person won't have enough receptors to lodge neuropeptides generated by optimistic or joyful states.

If our cells are daily and unconsciously bombarded by emotions (such as anger, fear, sadness, guilt, shame, etc.) generated by thoughts and belief patterns creating contractions, they will have less and less receptors able to manage the assimilation, nutrition, cleaning, and healing functions. People who daily give and receive love (to and from others and themselves) may enjoy more health at all levels, while those who spend most of the time judging, complaining, and blaming (others and themselves) will have many more physical, mental, or emotional problems. Love is, literally, what gives cells their vital force, while lack of love drains our vitality and health.

That which resists, persists. Resisting is attracting. This old maxim is very useful in understanding our problems. Cells are constantly being born, growing, and dying, which reflects the unrelenting change, transformation, and regeneration of the universe. We can flow with the changes that life puts in our way or we can resist them. Our work with cellular memory lets us observe that illnesses and dysfunctions we suffer are largely a direct consequence of our habit of resisting the flow of life as it manifests in our lives.

Cells seek naturally to transform. Accepting the flow of life and the consequent changes has a profound healing effect, because this attitude gives rise to inner and outer peace. This state deeply affects the cells, which instantly update the information contained in their physical, mental, emotional, and spiritual files. All useless information is removed from the cellular memory, to be replaced by new ways of being and acting. Techniques included in the protocols of CMR are designed to help produce these changes smoothly and deeply.

Cells are designed to clean up and eliminate patterns that are no longer useful, and to integrate new patterns that may awaken our ultimate potential. Cells get rid of that which they no longer need or want, and also fulfill this function energetically, eliminating useless resonances. Once the old toxic patterns have been discarded, they are replaced by newer ones that help us live in a healthier way.

The Energy Field Holds the Memory

Cells can only have memory when there is an energy field imprinting information on them. Although the human body is a wonderful creation, it stops functioning and becomes dead matter if we "unplug" it. The body we live in depends on us. We are its energy source; we are the "power" that sets in motion the bio-computer. All memory is in the energy field, and our vital force provides cells with the needed information as long as our bio-computer exists.

Old cultures and the indigenous wisdom accumulated during millennia knew of the existence of this powerful force that rules the entire universe. This vital force or "vital juice" has been called chi by the Chinese, ki by the Japanese, prana by the Hindu, and breath of life by Hebrews. All of them attempted to express the creative principle that makes everything exist. This is the principle that contains and sustains everything, that connects everything, and that has always existed, even before the beginning of life on Earth.

We can say that the human bio-computer has three main constituent parts: the physical body (the hardware), the belief system or program (the software), and the vital force (the power).

It was known very long ago that these constituent parts interact continuously and must be treated holistically in order to be in balance. In primitive cultures, the physician, the psychologist, and the priest were one and the same person. These roles began to differentiate over the centuries and now they are performed by different professionals. Today, when human beings are ill, they are treated as divided and compartmentalized entities, sometimes without any connection among these parts and without any chance to integrate them. The physician takes care of the body—though rarely in its entirety—while the psychologist and the priest (whatever their creed) attempt to take care of the soul. They don't usually interact, and if asked, do not often reach an agreement. But human beings today are no different now than those of ancient times, so that if they are consciously reeducated, they may still achieve the ability to reintegrate lost essence and unity.

Chinese philosophy teaches that vital force is magnetic and has a northern and a southern pole, which manifest in the body as positive and negative polarities. This pair is known as yin-yang. Yin energy flows from feet to head, while yang energy flows from head to feet. Neither is absolute; there is a bit of yin in the yang force and a bit of yang in the yin force. And the whole human bio-computer, at all levels and in its "files," has some positive elements in the negative parts and some negative elements in the positive parts. The positive and the negative flow constantly together and are necessary to one another in order to create a unified field of energy.

The files that have a positive charge are the result of all of our perceptions, beliefs, and decisions that helped and supported us until now and that inform us on a daily basis. This includes all natural, physical, mental, and emotional functions keeping us alive while we enjoy life and have healthy and creative expectations. These are the healthy beliefs and decisions that influence our choices and behaviors, and give support to a strong self-confident person: "I'm a healthy person," "I can," "I trust myself," "I have a right to establish limits," "I deserve to be happy." Those files that have a negative charge, generate weakness and insecurity: "Nobody loves me," "I don't trust my feelings," "I can't trust anybody," "I'm a failure," "I'm stupid," "There's no hope for me," and so on and so forth.

Related Research

"Though modern science still has a very primitive understanding of human beings, it is increasingly obvious that if we hope to achieve long-term or permanent results, the chemistry of emotions should

be a key factor in any therapeutic intervention. Every memory is recorded at the cell level, so that in treating stress problems originated by trauma or other psychosomatic or psychological conditions, we should carefully evaluate any method that may have a beneficial impact on destructive memory patterns."
—Thomas R. McClaskey, from The American Academy of Experts in Traumatic Stress.

There is an increasing amount of information coming out in the last decade about cellular memory. For example, if you search the Internet, Wikipedia (the free encyclopedia) says,

"Cellular memory is the hypothesis that such things as memories, habits, interests, and tastes may somehow be stored in all the cells of human bodies, not only in the brain. The academic organ transplant community accepts this notion as pseudoscientific [citation needed] and absurd [citation needed], as it has never been demonstrated in a scientific manner [citation needed]. There is also the fear that such notions may hinder organ donation [citation needed]. The suggestion arose following a number of organ transplants in which the recipient was reported to have developed new habits or memories. An article, "Changes in Heart Transplant Recipients that Parallel the Personalities of Their Donors," published in the Spring 2002 issue of the Journal of Near-Death Studies, reported stories of organ recipients who 'inherited' a love for classical music, a change of sexual orientation, changes in diet and vocabulary, and, in one case an identification of the donor's murderer."

They also say that the "citation needed" link was placed there because the Wikipedia's editor feels that the preceding statement is likely to be challenged, and therefore needs an in-line citation. Up to this day, no one has placed a citation to clarify those statements.

Paul Pearsall, M.D., an expert in psychoneuroimmunology and author of the book *The Heart's Code*, has studied the transference of memories through transplanted organs for many years. After interviewing more than 150 hosts of transplanted hearts and other organs, Pearsall concluded that the cells of live tissues have the capacity to remember.

Gary Schwartz, Ph.D., and Linda Russek, Ph.D., scientists working at the University of Arizona and coauthors of the book *The Living Energy of the Universe*, state the hypothesis that "all body systems store energy in a dynamic way, and the system formed with this information goes on living and evolving even after the supporting physical structure has already been destroyed." Schwartz and Russek believe this is how the donor's information may be consciously or unconsciously present in the transplanted organs or tissues. To read more about their research and the many case studies, check www.paulpearsall.com/info/press/3.html.

Candace Pert, professor at the Physiology and Biophysics Department of Georgetown University, who discovered the existence of neuropeptides in all the body tissues, suggests that thoughts and memories may remain unconscious, or become conscious through cell receptors, which pave the way to psychological connections between the memories, the organs, and the mind. In her book *Molecules of Emotion: The Science Behind Mind-Body Medicine*, she writes, "Mind isn't only in the brain, but all over the body." As an expert in the pharmacology of peptides, she adds, "Mind and body communicate through some chemicals known as peptides, which are in the brain and the stomach, the muscles, and the most important organs. I think one can have access to memory throughout the network created by peptides and receptors—for example, a memory linked to the pancreas and the liver, associated with food assimilation—and that those links can be transplanted from one person to another."

In his book *The Biology of Belief*, the American scientist and researcher Bruce Lipton M.D., founder of "epigenetics," says,

"We can no longer ignore the miraculous natural wisdom of the human body. At this moment, there are billions of undifferentiated embryonic cells designed to repair or replace damaged tissues or organs. The activity and fate of these regenerative cells are, however, epigenetically controlled. That means they are deeply influenced by thoughts and by the perception of the environment. For instance, our beliefs on old age may improve the way our undifferentiated cells function or interfere with them, thus causing either the regeneration or the decay of our physiology."

In another place, Lipton states,

"Just as the TV set captures waves transmitted through the air, so cell receptors capture information from our outer environment to build what we call our self. This information is under the form of energy radiation, and we receive and make it ours in the same way that we unload information from the Internet and save it in our computer's files. And just as we unload from the Web some information but not the whole of it, so we 'unload' only a limited range of all the information carried by the universal energy spectrum."

CHAPTER 7
Charges that Leave Traces

"Many behavior patterns of our daily life are the result of information decoded and stored at the cellular level. These patterns are largely benign and don't contribute significantly to the organism's dysfunction or destruction—as do illnesses, for instance. On the other hand, some of them are the materialized expression of information stored as a result of past traumatic experiences. In treating people who suffer traumatic disorders, we must take into account that their problem is the expression of that information decoded and stored in cells. For the therapeutic intervention to be helpful, it must focus on detecting, isolating, and decoding the cellular patterns produced by traumatic memory."
—Thomas R. McClaskey, *Decoding Traumatic Memory Patterns at the Cellular Level*

The Positive Emotional Charge (PEC)

In our universe, everything flows and the whole of creation is an endless dance of energy opposites that attract, complement, and are drawn together. To really understand cold, one must feel heat; to know the daylight, one must experience the darkness of night. None of these concepts can exist without the other. Thus, the male attracts and needs the female, and the positive pole attracts and needs the negative one.

We call this positive emotional charge to the vital force in movement. When a river freely flows toward the ocean, it nurtures and gives life to an infinite amount of organisms and vital manifestations. While the river keeps on flowing, all the ecosystems live and reproduce in healthy ways. Within the body-mind system there are also different channels that need to flow like a river in order to nourish all the rest of our systems and keep them alive and healthy:

- Air comes in and goes out through the bronchi.
- Blood flows through the arteries, veins, and capillary vessels, nurturing and cleaning.
- Lymph flows through the lymphatic vessels carrying away wastes and thus defending the entire organism.
- Nutrients go through the digestive system while they become part of the blood.
- Neurotransmitters go along neural pathways carrying information with them.
- The chi goes along the energy channels or meridians that form the energy body carrying the vital force.
- The vital force flows through the body-mind system as a whole, goes into the body and out of it, passing through the vortices of energy the Hindu call chakras, which connect the microcosm with the macrocosm.

This essential, creative vital force circulates in each and every manifested form of nature; it is fluid, fresh, and innocent. We can easily recognize it when we are moved by a flower, a baby, or a beautiful landscape.

Babies are almost wholly made up of positive energy charge. The newborn's energy field is highly sensitive and acts like a sponge. The degree of receptivity of her bio-computer is very large. It could be said that her only aim in life is to absorb all new information and experience, and to live all that life offers at each moment. The baby acts and feels according to the available vital force that flows freely through her system. In this state, there is no dam blocking the flow; "good" as well as "bad" sentiments are intensely felt and impersonally recognized. Babies are optimistic and have a great curiosity. Their parents are right when thinking that they must learn where there is danger; a baby's combination of innocence and candor lead them not to expect a negative event.

When we were babies, vital force flowed freely through our nervous system while our rational mind, almost idle at first, gradually gained space and activity as programming increased. In our civilization, the disproportionate amount of space our rational mind comes to occupy in adulthood suffocates, little by little, the emotions we so naturally expressed in our childhood. Thus, we gradually store the repressed vital force as negative emotional charge and energy contractions. We get used to this energy condition and think that suffering and pain are "normal." We come to think that we actually are composed of a pain body. We are unconscious victims and have one disappointment after the other, until the final one, which is death.

When the Negative Emotional Charge Displaces the Positive One

Has it ever happened to you that, while having a good time with your friends, you suddenly felt an inner tension because someone "turned negative"? Have you observed that it never happens the other way around? This is because people who feel negative emotions don't change their state if someone in the group is relaxed and joyful. However, it is often the case that a person who feels positive can change very quickly and unconsciously to feeling negative emotions. A positive emotional charge withdraws when a negative one is present because it naturally permits everything in. That's why babies are so sensitive and receptive to negative as well as positive emotions. Sometimes, an irrelevant negative event disturbs them so much that they feel really bad; they immediately complain and cry, since they absorb quickly the negative emotional charge of people around them.

Curiously enough, all human beings behave like this. The process begins in intrauterine life, when first the embryo and then the fetus absorb everything the mother feels and experiences, and afterward, during and after birth, the child goes on absorbing the energy resonances of the adults around her. During infancy, the child's rational mind begins to hold beliefs—or to imitate those of others—and makes decisions about herself and life in general, thus creating what we call a self-image, a kind of imaginary picture of herself. Our virtues and talents are, for the most part, the result of this unconscious process. At the same time and in the same way we get our deficiencies and shortcomings. With time, negative experiences, beliefs, and decisions accumulate in the body-mind system and give rise to the pain body.

Since all of us have been babies, all of us are essentially pure, positive emotional charge. Energy contractions have created a false identity in which we have lost that innate joy and suffer because of what we have created that isn't real. In other words, the pain body has replaced our original nature by suffocating the positive emotional charge. The latter is contracted, but still lives within us. If we want to find the way back to our light body and remember our original condition of a spontaneous, open, free-flowing being without our paralyzing self-images, fear of the future, or bitter resentments from the past, we need to become aware of our present condition and search for a way to go back to what we originally were. It is possible to return to the state of inner peace and joy we felt when we were babies. We must simply unlearn what we were taught was true in order to rediscover our essential being.

The Larger the Negative Charge, the Larger the Pain Body

At any moment, an intense negative emotional charge may trigger an apparent loss of vital force, actually trapped in the pain body. This is so because the positive emotional charge has "left the premises" and its space has been quickly occupied by false beliefs and negative decisions. Many people go through life having only a very small percentage of available vital forces, especially if they have already lived and suffered the consequences of the process I've just described, which I call the "inner civil war." This inner tension leaves a lot of casualties in its wake; above all, it leaves lack of authenticity and inner freedom. If the process is repeated again and again, there's an unconscious sensation of distancing and separation of the parts previously connected by positive emotional charge.

The larger the space gained by the pain body, the larger and heavier the inner sensation of discomfort, which in extreme cases makes the person feel that the burden is unbearable and that she doesn't want to go on living any longer. Another clear sign that our vital force is trapped in the pain body is when we are ashamed of ourselves or feel the need to hide. We don't want to, or can't, speak about some particular aspects of our life, as if we are keeping a large, destructive secret and cannot share or expose what we're living through. We feel ashamed, guilty, and fearful, and this causes an intense sensation of being separate from others. Shame, guilt, and fear are precisely the emotions that produce the largest number of contractions in the expanding, embracing energy field of the small child. These contractive feelings generate an inner split in us, and have been—and still are—failed strategies used by traditional religions and formal education with the intention to make us better human beings.

The percentage of contracted vital force that is no longer available to us determines the degree to which we can become dysfunctional. When the pain body controls the body-mind system, all kinds of physical or psychological imbalances and disturbances appear: weariness, fatigue, several types of pain and illness, compulsions and addictions, confusion, fear, anxiety, irritability and anger, depression, learning problems, alienation, procrastination, lack of will to make decisions, the feeling that life is meaningless, or simply the sensation of being overwhelmed and/or bored. The relative loss of vital force by energy contractions makes us feel incomplete or internally damaged. In this condition, we can come to believe that "something is wrong with us," that we have some congenital flaw, that we aren't valuable or good enough.

If we aren't aware of this separateness and negative self-judgment, we will feel anxious and have the need to have something—or somebody—that makes us feel well again. A bottomless hole will open in us and we will have to fill it with many kinds of substances (food, sweets, alcohol, tobacco, drugs), or with money, possessions, sex, personal success, power, recognition, or an idealized intimate relationship. In this state of lack of awareness, we delude ourselves into thinking that having those things will make us feel complete. When, after struggling and fighting, we eventually obtain them, we discover that the hole is still there, as deep and empty as before.

The Dangerous Game of Self-Condemnation: One of the Main Causes of Suffering

Is self-condemnation part of our original design? Can you imagine a baby beating up on himself saying, "Look at me, I'm fat," "What's wrong with me!" "I have no teeth and can't even walk," or "I can't do anything for myself, I can't even talk. I am so stupid! I can't stand myself!" It sounds absurd when we imagine a baby talking to himself like that. Yet tragically we do it to ourselves and each other all the time. A baby doesn't have a concept of self-hatred. We learn all these concepts by imitation when we are very young. We hear criticism and judgment and then we repeat them to ourselves and to others. We have to become convinced that if we love someone we have to criticize them. We begin to believe that the best way to motivate ourselves or another is through criticism. We believe that if we love our children, we need to show them their faults so that they become better human beings and then they will have a better life.

Is it true? In my experience, it's not. In my experience, this is the recipe for creating an insecure adult with low self-confidence and low self-esteem. Feelings of unworthiness, confusion, and lack of purpose can be expected in a child that is being judged and condemned on a daily basis. To counteract the effects of this programming, many of us have created a mask of power, efficiency, and happy smiles, and endlessly attempt to prod ourselves and others into believing that we are worthy when we accomplish the things we are told we are supposed to accomplish.

This programming detonates in us a resonance of chronic dissatisfaction, where we always need something else or someone else to complete us. We believe that if we had more money, a different body, a better job, a better relationship, a better house, or something more, then our lives would be complete. In an unconscious way, we search endlessly for success and wealth and that soul mate that never comes. The bottom-line message is: I am flawed, I am not enough, and something is missing in my life. The result is a deep state of emptiness and disconnection from life with a mixture of fear, anxiety, and frustration. This state even has a name approved by culture: it is called stress.

Once we learn self-condemnation, we live in stress. In addition, we are now part of an old cultural ritual that is always looking for what is missing in our lives and dismisses what we do have. Every moment we choose to take part in this ritual, we trade the power of abundant life for what we should or could have if things would be different. This creates a profound state of self-torture.

Each time we make a negative judgment about any aspect of ourselves—our physical appearance, mental traits, or emotional attitudes—the body-mind system (that is, essentially, positive emotional charge) goes immediately on the alert, since we're telling it that there is something wrong or at fault. At the same time, the system begins to search in its database of the past—the cellular memory— for something attuned with the error for which it has just been held responsible. These flaws can be remembrances of its current life or old genetic information, sometimes dating back many generations. When, through this scanning, the information is found, it is revived and brought to the present as evidence that there is truly "something wrong with me."

Since healing is an automatic and natural process, when a certain vibration takes place it is expected that the rest of the system—especially the rational mind, being the part that usually makes decisions—will support it. However, in our culture, our mind isn't ready to deal with cellular or ancestral memories, because it was given no information about that when it was programmed. In conclusion, each time we say there is something wrong with us, we raise the possibility of illness or unhappiness being revived from very old generational files. This negative self-judgment is a slow suicide as Lynn Grabhorn clearly states in her book *Excuse Me, Your Life Is Waiting*:

> "Self-condemnation, in whatever form, is a comfortable place to be when we don't want to take any responsibility for our life. We can meditate, sing chants, use crystals and incenses, make special exercises, or make affirmations proclaiming our eternal divinity, but if we go on judging ourselves, inner power and liberation will be mere words. No wish or desire can be fulfilled if you are in a state of self-disapproval. Then you can expect no abundance, inner well-being, or good health, and only a bit of joy."

CHAPTER 8

Healing and Transformation Are Possible: Some Practical Exercises

"There are two levels of pain: pain happening now and past pain still lingering in your mind and your body. The latter includes the pain you suffered in your childhood, caused by your lack of consciousness of the world you had been born into. That accumulated pain generates a negative energy field that conditions your mind and body in an extraordinary way. If you look at it like an unseen entity with its own will, you will be approaching truth. It is the pain body."
—Eckhart Tolle, *The Power of Now*

Pain Can Be Our Teacher and Guide

Through pain experiences, something in our deepest self can make its way to our consciousness and shine. Pain can be our ally, teacher, and guide. When consciously experienced, it is, paradoxically, a gate leading to the release of suffering.

Consciously lived, pain may lead us to a place that is like home, as if coming back to it. Most humans live in a state of unconscious suffering that is largely artificial. Sages and spiritual teachers of all time have said that this state is like daydreaming, a fantasy, a product of imagination.

Hinduism, for instance, calls it maya, the theatrical play the world is, a creation of gods, only a stage in a divine game. Regardless of the name we put on it, it's a state of being in which we make everything we can to be different from what we actually are. Thus, as under a hypnotic trance or a spell, we live our lives profoundly identified with that which is untrue. And we can remain in that state until the end of our life. Indeed, that's what happens with most humans.

EXERCISE

Take a moment to see the difference between the daydreaming state and being in the here and now. Breathe deeply and feel your body. How does it feel? What sensations do you have, and where? In what places is there relaxation or tension? (In case you're calm, try to see whether it's real calm or just drowsiness.) Feel your breath.

Now, while part of your attention is focused on the body sensations—your inner space—start to gradually recognize the outer space.

What is happening exactly within your body and out of it? Take hold of those perceptions, look at them for a moment, and feel them. Breathe.

This is the beginning of the "state of presence."

Transforming Pain

When one begins to know how to transform pain, what was a disturbance begins to become an opportunity. Physical pain, sadness, anger, and fear become possibilities for healing and having access to our true potential. This gives us the chance of awakening to a deeper sense of our inner self, which, paradoxically perhaps, needed us to be a bit unhealthy or unhappy in order to emerge in all of its eloquence. In order to transform pain we must feel in the moment the discomfort present in us. We may achieve this by submerging in the discomfort instead of fighting to get away from it. We must plunge toward the center of our discomfort with all our attention and presence, going to the depths of it without analyzing or interpreting where it comes from, why, or the reason for its existence. This is the essential core of the technique I've called pain body release (PBR). The individual results of this process are so amazing that it remains a mystery to me, but its practice is simple and easy to implement. I can honestly say that, after the awakening, life is not the same as before.

Learning the Language of the Body: Detecting the Pain Body

The pain body includes all that is perceived as uncomfortable or physically, mentally, or emotionally painful. When a small stimulus (such as a comment, a look, or a memory) provokes in us a disproportionate response, it is a signal that the pain body has been activated. Something has "pushed a button" and carries us to a place of panic, rage, or deep and inexplicable sadness. Has it happened to you at any time? In the following exercise, we'll make a partial outline of the pain body.

EXERCISE

Make a list of the persons or things that "push your buttons" in different areas of your life. For each of these triggers, answer the following questions:

- What thoughts come to my mind in that situation?
- What body sensations or feelings do I have when I think those thoughts?

(You may take a piece of paper and colored pencils or crayons, and draw a human silhouette to represent those sensations as well as you can.)

Now, answer these questions:
- If these sensations had a color, what would it be?
- If they had a weight, how heavy or light would they be?
- Are they cold or hot?
- In what area of your body are they localized?
- What other features do they have?

Returning to the Light Body

The expression "light body" describes what exists under the pain body, or more precisely, before it. The light body is what we naturally are. The less pain body there is at a given moment, the more light body we experience. The light body is the fundamental and basic energy that created us and gives us strength. It represents love, connection, optimism, trust, enthusiasm, and an infinite sense of freedom. It is a force flowing with life, not against it. And the good news is that it abounds. It's in the cycle of the seasons, in the orbit of the planets and the irrefutable order of the universe, in our heartbeat, and in the processes that heal our body. When that energy flows freely and unobstructed through all the body-mind system, we can have access to it. Perhaps you have already experienced that. We feel the light body when we simply enjoy something, when we are peaceful or calm without any motive, when we feel love without any apparent reason. The light body loves, shares, plays, dances, creates, is grateful, and enjoys music, children, tranquility, nature, and animals.

Looking at the open, innocent eyes of babies we can connect with what we really are in the depth of our being, under or before the layers of contracted energy that generated the pain body. If you spend some time watching babies, or in contact with nature or animals, and are present in what is happening to your body, you'll have a preview of your light body. You will notice that when the personality (or self-image) is absent, there's no resistance to the present moment, and things flow. Then the light body manifests itself, and this manifestation is always a blessing. We adults have many opportunities to feel the light body. A musician might experience it while composing a melody or playing a piece. In that case, the melody flows through her as if there was nobody there and the music was merely "played." Sometimes sportsmen and sportswomen experience this flowing when they feel that a game is played through them effortlessly. A couple may experience the light body when, for an instant, they forget any concept or feeling of separation and neither one of them knows where one body ends and the partner's begins. But the light body is not the piece of music, the match, or the surrendered lover. Its frequency is not a state of being that—like the pain body—might be triggered by an outer stimulus. It is the basic matrix of our human design and it cannot be lost or destroyed.

"I tell you the truth, unless you change and become like little children, you will never enter the kingdom of heaven." (Matthew 18:3)

It is no wonder that sages and masters of old have always praised children's innocence and have taken it as a reference for inner work and the development of consciousness. Even helpless, naked, and bald, even wet and sitting in a soiled diaper, even when they cannot keep their head upright or walk, babies are very close to the pure manifestation of the light body. The body-mind system of the newborn is highly sensitive and receptive. Her life is mainly dedicated to absorbing new experiences, and like a sponge, open to what life offers her at each moment. At one moment she's completely happy and five seconds later she's crying inconsolably. However, anything that emerges for the infant, whether "good" or "bad" feelings, are wholly felt and acknowledged, because there is no value judgment.

EXERCISE
1. Choose a time when you can relax and be quiet.
2. Close your eyes and imagine a place in nature where you feel at home. It can be a real place that you remember or an imaginary one. Visualize yourself there alone, with nothing to do and nobody to talk with. Breathe slowly.
3. Make a list of the sounds of that place, its smells, and the heavy or light atmosphere surrounding it. Take notice of your body.
4. How does your body feel in that place? How does your mind feel? Go on breathing slowly.
5. Stay there for a while, and see whether you experience your light body. How do you know that? Look for any feeling of peace, joy, lightness, or spaciousness. If you do, it's likely that you have begun to remember your own self.

The Pain Body Release (PBR) Process:
How to Transform Pain into Peace and Joy

When we grow up and become civilized adults, we tend to forget that we must allow our organic system time to process pain or discomfort naturally. In adulthood, we have already become masters in the art of resisting or eradicating it and, above all, we have forgotten how to transform it. If we want to recover the fresh, loving, and lively energy field we had when we were children, we must unlearn what we have learned, go back to square one, and establish new habits and ways of treating pain.

EXERCISE
1. Feel the physical pain or emotional discomfort that is present in you at this moment. You may also think of an experience that happened that left you feeling down.

2. Allow it to be, with all its force. Listen to the inner dialogue that sets in. If any thought comes to your mind, let it be.

3. Observe the mind's habit of avoiding discomfort, analyzing, or telling stories. Pay attention to your body and its sensations. Keep up your sensations and feelings such as they are. Watch in what part of your body the sensation is.

4. Let your body work through those energies while you witness the process. Observe what the body does (any inner sensation or feeling, any associated thought, etc.) without trying to control it. The pain body usually has various deep and thick layers of contracted life force. Perhaps you will experience waves of intense feelings and/or sensations alternating with periods of calm and relaxation.

5. Let the pendulum effect act as many times as you may need. You may change from discomfort to pleasure. Trust the natural intelligence of your body. You are neither one extreme of the pendulum or the other, but the neutral point permitting the pendulum to be. You are that which witnesses.

6. The above may take from a couple of minutes to a half an hour or longer. After entering the pain body, take some time alone to integrate what you experienced. You may lay on the floor or the bed for a while, and then write it down in your notebook.

To transform the energy contractions we call pain, we need attention and presence. When we pay attention to what we feel is uncomfortable or painful, we can become more conscious of sensations and feelings, as well as our thought patterns and the beliefs that feed them. In such a case, we can begin to unravel them. This is an extremely simple process, though it may seem difficult at first, partly for lack of practice, but mainly because we've been trained to judge, resist, and fight the uncomfortable or painful.

Perhaps the creation of the pain body took all our life. The transformation of the contractions can be instantaneous.

I see the pain body release as an uncontrollable forest fire, and the state of presence as a wind spreading that wildfire. The more present we are, the more transformational that fire is. Large areas of lying and fear, of shame and self-condemnation, are laid waste in its path, giving place to what has been there forever, waiting to be experienced and recognized: our true self. Life—that brief interval between birth and death—can be missed entirely in the daydreaming and fantasy state created by our rational mind, while a wonderful world is changing around us at every moment, even when we are distracted trying to review the past or predict the future. However, just as a drifting boat benefits from the beams of a lighthouse, we can experience in our body very intense sensations if we shake ourselves, even temporarily, from the dream in which we are immersed and go to encounter the powerful "now." When we feel physical or emotional pain and pay attention to the area of our body that is thus activated, we take ourselves to the present moment. In this way, pain returns us to life, which is always happening now, at this precise instant. This is a frequently asked question in our workshops: should we, perhaps, create more pain to free ourselves from suffering?

But, no, there is enough pain in our lives and around us; there is no need to create even more. Pain is like an alarm clock blaring louder the more we want to ignore it. And if we hush it up resorting to some of the numerous strategies we know, the noise will start again some time later, probably much more intensely. What you resist persists, and in fact, intensifies. Pain can be our spiritual alarm clock. "Wake up!" it seems to tell us, "It's time to get up and live a real life." Sometimes, an intense, deep pain is like a gift liberating us once and for all from suffering. The mystics and spiritual teachers of all time have pondered about the transformational power of pain, and taught that both physical and emotional pain may be excellent opportunities for us to be in touch with what is alive in us and to experience what we really are while being open to that which lies beyond the body.

EXERCISE

Pay attention to what is alive in you and in your body for a while. Just perceive every sensation, without trying to fix or change anything. Be aware of your posture, and of the tense and relaxed areas. In case you feel uncomfortable somewhere, acknowledge it. Perhaps you have read this book until now without thinking at all how your body feels. Even at this moment, you may be reading with the aim of avoiding a painful or unpleasant sensation.

Take a minute to note that uneasiness, be it big or small. Be curious, put all your attention on it, and feel it, really feel it.

Now, ask yourself the following question: what is actually experiencing within you?

Do not lose your connection with your body sensations. Concentrate upon that experience without changing it. In other words, be the experience at this very moment.

Thus focused, the body can be a gate to reality. Unfortunately, many spiritual teachings overlook or deny the body instead of concentrating upon it to embrace the life that is happening there. And, as we already know, fighting it inevitably brings with it resistance, and resistance produces more and more suffering, making it last. Pain is a symptom, a warning about a deeper phenomenon. It always has a message for us. When the message is delivered, pain goes away.

We have to face it and listen to what it has to tell and teach us.

Experiences with PBR

"You are not your thoughts. Thoughts are only a current flowing through your mind. You don't have to struggle to control them. What you must do is become a passive observer of any event occurring in your mind's theater. If you were in your seat at a theater you could see how one actor after the other crosses the stage. Were one of them to play the role of a cruel monster, you wouldn't be scared. Were another to announce with a loud booming voice that 'there's no way out,' you would know it's a performance and would not feel in danger."

—Vernon Howard

CMR consists of two primary processes: pain body release (PBR) to clear blocked energy and dissipate accumulated pain, and neural net repatterning (NNR) to examine and remove the beliefs that created the pain in the first place, beliefs such as "I am not worthy" or "I am not lovable." Together they create a synergistic process that helps us return to our original resonance of peace, joy, and authenticity. Paradoxically, through entering the pain we rediscover our joy.

Below are some examples of the pain body release process applied by CMR students. In the next chapter we'll explain the NNR technique and show some real cases.

All sessions are designed to unfold from the facilitator's deeply held state of presence that assists the person in reaching his own wisdom stored in his own being. By fully entering his own presence, the depths of his own being, the facilitator of the PBR process assists the person in moving out of the details of his problematic "story" and into fully allowing whatever comes forward in the body in response to the story. The person may feel pressure, heat, tension. He may have memories or images come forward. The facilitator helps the person stay out of the thoughts about what the problem is and stay with what happens in the body, encouraging the person to intensify any physical response that occurs. This allows the person to tap into his own vast intelligence to heal and transform any challenge through locating the resonance by following the pain and then releasing it through the alchemy of the person's own wisdom. What often emerges is the sense of release, calm and peace, of entering the light body.

Transforming the Pain Body

What follows are somewhat longer experiences reported by some of my students during their training as CMR facilitators. There are two voices: one is the person's and the other one is that of the student who facilitated the session.

Four Real Case Examples

PBR Experience #1: The person said she was very nervous because she was filing an application for a doctorate abroad. She had decided to do it one year ago but couldn't begin the formalities for it because she had no money. Now they had answered her favorably, and the decision made her feel both nervous and exalted. She is twenty-seven years old and this is the third session with her.

Since she had some experience with the CMR process and she already knew more or less how to enter into the body, she shuts her eyes and breathes. I ask her to remain with the feeling of nervousness for a while. Then she has a memory of her school time. She says she gets nervous because of different things, but all are the same, and that her nervousness is a need to defend herself (benefit). I ask her again, "What is the positive side of your need to defend yourself?" She answers, "It makes me feel safer, more energetic, and able to better express myself." In previous sessions, she had never expressed any emotion; she had only sensations. Besides, this time she puts her hand on her belly. I ask her, "What are you feeling now?" and she answers, "I feel disconnected. I have always hated my name; it was very unusual among Jews." Then she talks about her school.

She says she isn't free to say what she wants, she isn't respected. She's afraid of being judged. This fear makes her feel a heavy burden [she points to her belly] and she asks for help. She lies on the floor, tucks her legs back to a fetal position, and takes her head in her hands. Then she curls up on her stomach. She doesn't feel the burden in the belly any longer, says energy is going up and down very quickly through her spine, and says that it's disagreeable. She regards her spine as a mountain range, a very strong whole. The strength becomes vibration and reaches her right knee. "It's out of control." Then, the vibration feels good— she likes it. She remains this way for a while and then feels a warm, uncomfortable sensation in her left knee. It stings. Warmth increases and reaches a point at which it turns cold. She's confused. The warmth in her left knee goes to her right knee. I ask her to intensify what she feels in her right knee. It stings, it burns. She frowns for the first time, commenting that there's still an oscillation from warmth to coldness in her left knee, and says, "They have different rhythms." I ask her to acknowledge that and, if possible, try to notice how her legs feel at the same time. "It's something unknown and known," she says. I ask her to allow this sensation of something unknown and known and give in completely to it. She begins to move slowly, her legs pounding the floor until all her body is shaking. Her arms also pound the floor. Her hands move desperately along the whole body. She shakes her head. Every movement is more and more strong. She's completely plunged into constant movement, with no rhythm or direction. Then she begins to slither more quietly as a serpent. I ask what is happening; she answers, "I don't know ... my body simply moves ... it's out of control." "How do you feel?" "Fine, I feel more like myself."

Up to this point, we've had a one-hour session. I ask her to acknowledge that fine state and that, while allowing her body to move, she also permit that each of her cells recognize that "fine feeling." Her body begins to move more slowly. "What are you feeling?" "I feel good. I've got a tingling sensation in my hands."

I give her some more time to feel and recognize what is happening, and I begin to close the session with words related to the Vast Intelligence. Her body gets calmer. Her shoulders and arms still shake from time to time. Her face changes. (Not that it was tense, but it is now more relaxed.) I realize then that those words about the Vast Intelligence are deeper than simply "being well."

At the end of the session she felt radiant. And she recognized again what she had felt before when I asked her to review her idea of not being respected, not being free, having a need to defend herself, and being nervous. "Now all that makes no sense any longer," she said. She also commented that, in her view, she hadn't entered into her body so quickly this time. It had been different. She only entered into it after a while, and this time she had moved a lot. I explained to her that we had previously done NNR but now we had done PBR.

After two days, she called me to express her gratitude and to tell me that now she was feeling very calm and certain about her decision. I feel very glad when I see that somebody allows herself to experience her feelings.

PBR Experience #2: This one-hour session is the fourth one with this forty-eight-year-old woman. She is feeling a lot of stress because of her financial situation. She was a professional for about a decade until she grew tired of it. Since a year ago she has stopped practicing her profession and is looking for a change in careers.

She says, "I have many debts and I have no choice. In the process of accepting being a woman, I feel I have a sort of prohibition against being a productive person. A woman, it is said, is a dependent person. She is at home. She is a housewife. Housewives don't provide for others. They're provided for by their husbands. Now, I have to earn a living, and there're no money sources available."

I tell her, "Shut your eyes and just imagine this woman without a coin, with no money, not even for eating." She answers, "I begin to revolt against it, and I have the sensation that my body gets bigger. I resist, I don't want this, and it's like going to the extreme of having to be more of a rotten swine than you. Look, I'm bigger than you and I can ride roughshod over you so that you fulfill my demands. I don't want that. There's no need to ride roughshod over someone in order to demand that one's own rights are respected. Is there any reason to ride roughshod over somebody's rights?"

"What do you feel about all this?"

"I feel greatly annoyed and sad."

She begins to cry. I tell her, "Intensify it." She cries intensely. I tell her, "You're doing pretty fine," and she cries even more strongly. "Imagine the worst of scenarios."

"I'm completely cornered."

"What do you feel?"

"Much sadness and worry. It's as if I don't exist for others."

"Please, exaggerate your sadness and worry. Cry more strongly, more intensely, with a profound worry." Suddenly, she begins to calm down.

"I'm alone, alone with myself. I feel as if I was like a phoenix and rise from my own ashes, from what I actually am."

"Allow yourself to feel it from the depth of your cells. Breathe deeply." Now she looks placid.

"I feel my body full of energy and light."

"Go on breathing and enjoying it." She sweetly and pleasantly smiles. "Scan your whole body with this new energy you have. From that place, take a new look at the person that believed that being a woman can't be productive. What do you feel?"

"I can see and feel it isn't true. It's a senseless lie."

"Now feel it in your body. You're listening to me while you're sitting on the chair, feeling the heaviness and temperature of your body, the rubbing of your clothes on your skin. Take a deep breath and go back to your adolescence, or even further back, when you learned that belief."

"How strange, I'm just seeing it. It's Mom when she was a little child. She's crying a lot. She's afraid because her mother is dying and they don't have a red cent."

She cries intensely and tucks her legs back as in a fetal position. "Intensify that as much as you can till you reach the worst of scenarios."

"My mother has died …"

She goes on crying inconsolably for a while. "Allow yourself to take that infinite pain and turn it into something more serious." After that she says, "I'm even worse than before. I remain completely alone and helpless."

"Put your hand on your forehead and speak to your mom."

"Mom, I've been so close to you that I've even felt your infinite pain when you were four and lost your mother. When I was in your womb, I got your feelings, your pain, your paralysis, and took charge of all your emotions. I've felt what was yours as if it were mine. I merged myself with you. I was professionally paralyzed to stay at home like you, a housewife. Mom, now I'm giving back to you these sentiments. They are yours. I return them to you. Please take them and take charge of them so that I can take charge of mine and be liberated while liberating you. So I'll be seen as a separate woman who is different from you. Let me wish that you die as the mother I couldn't part with, the mother I have merged with …"

She looks quite calm. She peacefully cries.

"What is happening now?"

"I feel deeply moved because I feel integrated for the first time ..."

She says, "I feel extremely well. What I liked most ... was everything. Everything was most important. It was fantastic to let go of my mother's energy, which had me trapped. To feel my own energy and her courage was very valuable, as valuable as gold. Since I recognize my work, everybody may recognize it, and one way to recognize it is by paying for it. It's nice, beautiful. It's also beautiful to be able to share it with everybody."

PBR Experience #3: The person is my twenty-one-year-old daughter. We had this session a month and a half ago. (It was the second time I applied the process.) She was overweight and this problem became more acute when she separated from her father. I had helped her with conscious breathing several times, and she reported it had been very useful. Now she wanted to lower her level of anxiety. She had learned how to manage food and was careful in choosing low-calorie foods, but in critical times she became very anxious and ate a lot. She wanted to reach the root of her difficulty.

She had some difficulty in getting in touch with her body. She spent around fifteen minutes in an inner scanning and reviewing. I told her to take all the time she needed and make a thorough review. At one point, a pressure she was feeling on her back made her lean forward and adopt a fetal position. After that, she began to have pains in her limbs and wasn't able to move her body at all. Her respiratory tract was occluded or "blocked." I told her to allow everything, to go on breathing, and to intensify it.

Then she began to make contact with the image of her maternal grandmother, who had taken care of her and spoiled her. Her grandmother had died three years ago. Then she had been cared for by a nurse, while both of us went to work, because of a painful illness that left her disabled her last eight years. When her grandmother died, my daughter became very sad, but she had never actually worked through her mourning.

At that moment, when she says she is "blocked," I suggest that she plunge into what she's feeling, and she starts crying. She cries very deeply for ten or fifteen minutes, while I keep her company. After she stops crying, she begins to make contact with a very strong sensation in her stomach. She feels nauseous and begins to salivate a lot. I talk to her about the wisdom of the body, and tell her that she can enter into the experience and allow it as she goes on breathing. She says it's like vomiting energy elements. She also says she's hungry, and cries. She reports that each time she feels anxious or anguished for something her mind interprets as a loss, she gets hungry. She remains silent for a while, and then she reports a sensation of well-being and seeing bright, brilliant colors in multiple pastel shades. She smiles, opens her eyes, and embraces me.

I suggest that she take a further look into herself. She answers that she feels as if her body is reconnecting. I conclude by reading the full text on the Vast Intelligence. After a moment of rest, she begins to write a report. I leave her alone.

She said she never imagined that she could discover so many things and that she found the process fascinating. She hasn't eaten when she felt anxious since then. She realized that it wasn't the separation from her father that had affected her so much, but rather the fact that she had to coexist with him, because he had drinking problems and it had been too hard for her when they all lived together.

PBR Experience #4: This forty-one-year-old woman had been doing therapy after her mother's death. In a special session with the therapist, she found out that her father had raped her since she was a small child (perhaps two years old) and continued to do that repeatedly until she was around twelve. This finding created a hard emotional impact upon her, since she had completely erased from her mind the sexual abuse episodes.

She reported having rejected her father without any explanation, and being afraid and resentful of men generally. "The only person that I've been involved with in my life mistreated me all the time."

This person enters very quickly into the pain body. At first, she cries deeply for ten minutes. I invite her to allow her crying and reassure her by telling her that her body is very wise, and that this is what is needed at this moment. When I ask, "What do you feel?" she answers that she feels very angry. I give her a towel to wring it. "Where?" She answers, "In my belly, all through my body." She begins wringing the towel and her fingers take the form of claws.

She puts much strength into the process. She tears up the towel cutting it into pieces while crying desperately. She pounds upon anything she happens to find around her. I give her a cushion. Suddenly, she stops and remains expectant, as if watching something, round-shouldered and still with her clawlike hands. I repeatedly tell her to get in touch with her body and emotions, but she says she's afraid of that. She sees a girl hiding somewhere (she goes on crying and moaning), and someone is looking for her to harm her. I constantly ask her to express what she feels and where she feels it. I invite her to allow those feelings, and to tell me what she feels when allowing them. She reports feeling strong emotions, as well as intense pain in her arms and legs, a paralysis in the legs, and involuntary movements in several areas of her lower limbs. I suggest that she allow them, exaggerate them, and remind her that her body is very wise and knows what needs to be healed, so that the only thing we can do is to permit it.

She says she feels a lump in her throat and that she wants to scream. I give her permission to scream as loudly as she wants. After a while, I ask her about the lump and invite her to breathe into it, but she says it's too strong and can't be unleashed. I ask her to describe it. "Who put the lump there?" She says, while crying heartbreakingly, that her mother's and father's images are emerging. Then she adopts the fetal position, groans, and tells me she doesn't want to talk. She's afraid and wants to be silent. I suggest that she allow the silence. It lasts for around ten minutes. I keep her company with my silent and loving presence. After that, I introduce the concept of the Vast Intelligence.

She says she's very tired. (I'm tired too.) I tell her to rest, to permit herself a rest, and to recognize what she's done. After resting, she wrote something down (she didn't want to share it with me). She said she was feeling much better and wanted me to embrace her. I did it lovingly. She said that she felt as if a big burden had been taken away. She smiled and laughed. She was obviously glad. I had been very present and on the alert during the entire session. Perhaps I invested too much energy in it, because at the end I was quite tired, though happy with the result. The person still had some doubts, though, curiously enough, she looked radiant.

In my experience the pain body release process allows people to free up blocked energy that is negatively impacting their physical and emotional well-being. Because the facilitator also takes time to educate the person in this process, it is very empowering. Within a relatively short number of sessions, the person is able to apply the process to his or her own experience whenever any upset is present. The process becomes a long-term tool they can use to liberate themselves from their problematic stories and to enter more fully into their authentic self.

Below you will find the link to access a video where you can see the PBR process in action. Please leave your comments in our forum.

http://www.cellularmemory.org/landing/pbrexample.html

CHAPTER 9
Neural Net Repatterning (NNR)

Exposing the Belief System—A Parable.
Once upon a time there was a large pond that became lifeless for no apparent reason. It used to be the most beautiful pond in this public park and everyone was very proud of it. Boulders and many flowers and trees surrounded it. The geese and ducks would raise their chicks there while sharing the place with all sorts of multicolored birds and fishes. Parents would bring the children to visit the pond and spend hours enjoying the aromas, the sounds, and the scenery.

No one knew what really happened, but in a few months, the waters turned dark and stinky and the life of the pond gradually disappeared. All the fish died and the birds left, probably looking for a healthier environment. The authorities in charge of the park were very confused, not knowing what to do, and decided to ask for help from a couple of experts. After studying the situation thoroughly, the first expert said, "If we manage to bring the fresh clean water from the nearby spring, in a few months we'll have the waters renovated and the life will come back to the pond. That's my advice."

The other expert thought for a moment and, shaking his head, said, "I don't think that will solve this situation. We don't know the cause of the problem here. We may have contamination coming from different sources: dark waters, chemicals, you name it. What's killed the life of the pond once will continue doing it if we don't stop the cause. I suggest investigating the water composition to find out what is causing the pollution. After that we'll need to empty out the pond, fix the source of toxicity, and then refill it with clean, fresh water. That'll take care of the problem once and for all. That is my advice."

So, which advice would you follow?

I always ask this question during the events that I offer, and unanimously people go for the second choice. And I agree with them. Even though it may be more work at the beginning, it will pay in the long run.

The PBR process will help us get rid of the toxicity accumulated in us and we'll feel much better after it. But this will not be enough. We must also release the thinking patterns associated with the beliefs that created the pain in the first place.

In my experience working with cellular memory release (CMR), I have learned that the things we believe create feelings in us, and those feelings create our reactions, habits, and behaviors. For instance, let's bring out one of the beliefs that most civilized adults have to deal with now: *I am unworthy.*

This is a toxic thought that the more we believe it, the more we may feel sad, alone, and frustrated. As a result, an undesired behavior of self-exclusion and shyness may overcome us.

In some other people, the same thought may create resentment and an uncontrollable need to prove themselves, causing irritable and bossy behavior. We can see this version in many people in charge of others, like parents, teachers, managers, or bosses.

The repetition of the feelings and the undesired habit or behavior affects our energy field with what we call negative emotional charge (NEC). The accumulation of NEC in the cells of our body is the source of the pain body that we've been discussing in depth in previous chapters. As we said, the pain body feeds our minds and an inner dialogue happens. This is what I call the inner commentary, a voice that tells me what life is like and what I should do about it based on past experiences. Because the pain body has its own way to perceive life, it distorts what we see and we no longer see what is really happening; we see through the colored glasses of the pain accumulated in us.

In summary, toxic beliefs create uncomfortable feelings. Uncomfortable feelings create undesirable habits and behaviors. The repetition of undesirable behaviors creates NEC in the cells. Accumulated NEC creates the pain body and the resulting inner dialogue. The inner dialogue feeds the image of myself with its toxic thoughts. The toxic thoughts become beliefs when we believe them.

Beliefs are just our strong opinions. They are not real. Believing them makes them real. Because of beliefs, we make decisions about our own life and other people's lives. These opinions control us and many times we may kill others or ourselves because of them. The mind is an amazing device and it will follow exactly the thoughts that are programmed in it. If our mind holds toxic beliefs, it will be difficult for us to have an enjoyable life journey. The mind's way is to do things in the "right" way and the right way is always following what it believes.

I've seen that many times we prefer to be right than to be happy. We prefer to be right than to be free. Our mind's programming tells us that there is only one right way to do things and if we always believe the programming without any investigation, it will lead us to the same spot again and again. If we want to change undesirable habits and behaviors, we need to investigate and change the source of the toxicity that always resides in the beliefs that we believe.

EXERCISE

Read the following list and rate yourself from 1 to 10—1 being "I don't agree with this statement at all," and 10 being "I agree 100 percent with this statement."

I advise you not to stop while you are reading the statements. This exercise becomes more effective the less you analyze the different statements. Read each one and immediately rate yourself. Move to the next as soon as possible.

1. _____ I am responsible for other people's feelings.

2. _____ I am not worthy.

3. _____ My life is difficult.

4. _____ I have to be unhappy when other people are unhappy.

5. _____ Love equals pain.

6. _____ I have to hide parts of my body.

7. _____ I need sex in order to feel loved.

8. _____ I am not important.

9. _____ Love is more important than money.

10. _____ Feeling equals weakness.

11. _____ I have to tolerate anything in order to not be alone.

12. _____ Love without money has no worth.

13. _____ I have to be anxious in order to be productive.

14. _____ Intimacy without sex has no worth.

15. ____ I have to change my body in order to be accepted.

16. ____ I must hide my sadness if I want to be loved.

17. ____ We shouldn't live our life without a partner.

18. ____ I am ashamed of my past.

19. ____ Money is the source of all evil.

20. ____ My life would be different if my body was different.

21. ____ I have to say yes when I want to say no in order to be accepted.

22. ____ Intimacy is a scary thing.

23. ____ It's OK to be rude with the people I love.

24. ____ The older you get the less healthy you are.

25. ____ I have to please others in order to be approved.

26. ____ I feel ashamed of my body.

27. ____ I have to control my emotions.

28. ____ Women don't know how to manage money.

29. ____ Poor people go to heaven.

30. ____ I have to lie to protect myself.

31. ____ I feel responsible for other people's problems.

32. ____ I am not a healthy person.

33. _____ Wealthy people are unhappy.

34. _____ I am not good enough.

35. _____ Bad things always happen to me.

36. _____ I am worthy as long as I make money.

37. _____ I cannot be alone.

38. _____ I cannot trust anybody.

39. _____ I don't trust rich people.

40. _____ I usually attract people that betray me.

41. _____ I am a loser.

42. _____ Real love only happens in the movies.

43. _____ Nobody recognizes me.

44. _____ I cannot be myself if I want to be included.

45. _____ I am weak when I feel emotions.

46. _____ I feel guilty for my past.

47. _____ You cannot make money doing what you love.

48. _____ My problems are always their fault.

49. _____ I will be happy the day I have a lot of money.

50. _____ Everybody lies to me.

51. _____ I feel stupid most of the time.

52. _____ God doesn't like money.

53. _____ Life isn't safe.

54. _____ I have to have sex to get financial support.

55. _____ If I criticize the people I love they will have a better life.

56. _____ Money is not important in life.

57. _____ I have to get angry to get things done.

58. _____ If I worry for others, they will know that I love them.

59. _____ I have to lie to get what I want.

60. _____ My body's desires complicate my life.

61. _____ I have to lie to maintain harmony in my relationships.

62. _____ If I am wealthy, people will criticize me.

63. _____ It's better to be a good person than to have money.

64. _____ It's impossible to be friends and lovers at the same time.

65. _____ People love and take care of me when I suffer.

66. _____ I have to get angry to set boundaries.

67. _____ Couples get bored after several years together.

68. _____ I have to dress and look the way others expect me to.

69. _____ My intimate life has to follow society's rules.

70. _____ I am ashamed of the sexual fantasies I have.

71. _____ I don't deserve to be happy.

72. _____ Those that have money don't have love and vice versa.

73. _____ I know what is right for the people I care about and love.

74. _____ I have to defend myself when someone criticizes me.

75. _____ I have to be right.

76. _____ It's very important what others think of me.

77. _____ I don't know how to have fun.

78. _____ I don't trust my own decisions.

79. _____ I cannot be happy when so many people are suffering in the world.

80. _____ I don't know how to be spontaneous.

81. _____ God will punish me for my past.

82. _____ I don't trust myself.

83. _____ My body and my mind are dirty.

84. _____ I cannot be spiritual and have money at the same time.

85. _____ Parents always know what is best for their children.

86. _____ I have to keep my distance from people.

87. _____ I have to be anxious to show that I care.

88. _____ If I show my frustration, they won't like me.

89. _____ I don't need love.

90. _____ I have to be generous and loving even when I don't feel it.

91. _____ I am afraid of others' reactions if I say what I really think.

92. _____ If I am authentic, I cannot be compassionate at the same time.

93. _____ I cannot ask for what I want.

94. _____ If I become wealthy, I will lose all my friends.

95. _____ If I set boundaries they will think I am rude.

96. _____ When I am compassionate, people take advantage of me.

97. _____ People get hurt when I say my truth.

98. _____ I have to sacrifice myself for others.

99. _____ I'll never be healed.

100. _____ Life is pain and effort.

101. _____ Wealthy people won't get into heaven.

102. _____ I am so tired of this life!

103. _____ I shouldn't be on this planet.

104. _____ If I am professionally successful I will abandon my family.

105. _____ I don't trust the people around me.

106. _____ I don't believe in friendship.

107. _____ I don't have any control over my life.

108. _____ If I show my feelings, I will be manipulated.

109. _____ My life is wrong for me.

110. _____ I'll always be angry.

111. _____ They will think I am dishonest if I am wealthy.

112. _____ They will always betray me.

113. _____ Life is such a burden!

114. _____ It's not safe to make changes.

115. _____ I wish I never had to deal with money.

116. _____ If people really knew me, they wouldn't like what they see.

117. _____ I am a monster.

118. _____ I have secrets that I cannot tell anybody.

119. _____ We don't need money if we have love in our lives.

120. _____ My parent (or parents) are the cause of all my problems.

121. _____ Nothing ever happens for my benefit.

122. _____ I am unable to ask for what I want sexually.

123. _____ Relationships are not for me.

124. _____ I am a good giver and a bad receiver.

125. _____ There is something wrong or broken in me.

126. _____ If you love me, you must be stupid!

127. _____ I don't have any time left for my family.

128. _____ I am not a good parent.

129. _____ I am ugly.

130. _____ I am fed up with my life.

131. _____ Others know better than me.

132. _____ I have to smile even when I feel horrible inside.

133. _____ This negativity will never end.

134. _____ I am not a lucky person.

135. _____ Aging brings disease.

136. _____ I am indispensable.

137. _____ I don't accept the way I am.

138. _____ The only reason to work is to make money to survive.

139. _____ I am not trustworthy.

140. _____ To be responsible, I have to worry.

141. _____ I should be happy all the time.

142. _____ I prefer to be on my own.

143. _____ I feel trapped with no way out.

144. _____ I have to get angry to be respected.

145. _____ I don't belong.

146. _____ Other people belong but I don't.

147. _____ I'll always be depressed.

148. _____ No one will be able to help me.

149. _____ Some stress is good for you.

150. _____ I am not at home on Earth.

151. _____ I cannot trust humans.

In the spaces below, list any beliefs you recognize within yourself that have not already been stated.

152.

153.

154.

155.

156.

157.

158.

159.

160.

161.

162.

163.

164.

EXERCISE

As you read the various exercises, you may find yourself feeling some resistance to doing some of them. If so, know that you can always come back to them at another time. Trust yourself and the process.

Three Steps to Start Changing Old Habits and Behaviors

Choose a statement that has a lot of charge for you. It might be one of those that you marked with a 10. Follow the steps below to start defusing the charge that is holding the belief alive and well. Remember that beliefs create feelings and feelings create the behaviors. As we could see in the pond's metaphor, adding clean water to the toxic pond won't help much. That is one of the reasons I've found that affirmations hardly ever work.

In the CMR process I teach that there are three steps to changing undesirable patterns:

1. Awareness of the pattern we want to change (draining the toxic waters).
   • What happens in me when I am repeating this pattern?
   • How do I behave?
   • What do I do or say?
   • What do I not do or say?
   • What is my posture like?

- What is my inner dialogue, or what is my mind saying?
- How do I treat myself and others?

2.

a) Deactivation of the pattern in the body (finding the toxic source). Find the belief behind the pattern.
   - What happens in my body when I am believing it?
   - What happens in my body?
   - What sensations do I have? Where?
   - What feelings do I have? Where?
   - What posture or movements can I make when I feel like this?
   - Do I have any images or memories coming?

b) Deactivation of the pattern in the mind.
   - What beliefs are behind this pattern?
   - Where are they coming from?
   - How did I learn them? From whom?
   - What would my life be like without the belief?
   - Is it true? Is it really 100 percent true?
   - Is there any evidence that it is no longer true?

3. Reprogramming the new pattern (filling the pond with clean, fresh water).
   - What will happen if I update this programming?
   - What am I afraid of when I think of this pattern going away?
   - What will happen if I no longer have this belief?
   - What beliefs do I need to have to support the new pattern?
   - What would my life be like if I live it from the new set of beliefs?

Journal about all these questions and get clearer about the painful patterns and the toxic beliefs that have created them. It is very important to realize that they are no longer true for you. Maybe they were useful twenty or forty years ago when you were a child, but they no longer apply to you. Also journal about the new beliefs that support you in your present experience and in what way your life would change if you use them.

An excellent way to support your inner work and become more aware of the patterns is to journal about any challenges, negativity, conflict, etc., a few times a week. Then review your notes a few times a month, checking to see if any new component emerges.

They are much easier to recognize after journaling about them. To get deeper into this, explore the neuropathways behind the beliefs using the NNR technique explained below.

To get free access to more exercises like this one, please go to www. cellularmemory.org.

Case Examples Using NNR

Modern science has compared the human brain with an extraordinary center of command that processes data and directions coming from different places in the organism. Our brain houses billions of cells called *neurons*; it is said that there are as many neurons in the nervous system as stars in our galaxy. These neurons join in *neural pathways*, and all neural pathways constitute the *neural net*. The neural net is activated by electrochemical impulses generated in the brain. This information flows through the nervous system from one extreme to the other and I called it "info-energy." It travels from cell to cell at a very high speed. Among other components, it includes *neurotransmitters*.

Researchers say that neurotransmitters are like electrochemical messengers used by cells to communicate with each other. A simple thought may trigger an enormous amount of neurotransmitters. When one neuron sends its neurotransmitters to the others with which it is in contact, an inner experience in the form of sensations and emotions is produced, and the relation between neurons gives rise to the so-called neural pathway. When there is a thought, the neural net is activated and we experience an inner feeling or a physical sensation. But if the same stimulus is sent again and again carrying the same kind of info-energy, the neurons develop a very close relationship among themselves, and these intensify over time. Dendrites and the axon, which are like the arms of the neuron, stretch out trying to make contact with an increasing amount of adjacent neurons, so that eventually the neural pathways are strengthened.

Every known behavioral pattern, habit, addiction, and compulsion follows this neural-energy pattern, and the repetition of these patterns creates an energy *resonance* in us. A resonance is an unconscious pattern that manifests outwardly the same reality with which it internally resonates. If we repeatedly use the same thought patterns every day, those inner relationships are strengthened and the same emotional reactions are produced over and over again. As a consequence, we attract in the outside world those frequencies with which we internally resonate. Through the repetition of the same patterns, a self-image is created in response to the physical or emotional injuries we have suffered in the past. What we must realize is that it is simply an image; it isn't, hasn't ever been, and won't ever be *real*. Other names used to describe this same concept are *ego, false personality, false self,* or *mask.* This self-image is composed of numerous beliefs that control us and that we mistake for reality.

After three or four years practicing and training others in PBR, I noticed that for some people it was not working in the way it was expected. Regardless of how much pain body they were accessing and moving during the sessions, there was always more pain and discomfort coming in. In other words, I felt like we were emptying water out of the pond and more toxic water was coming in from some unknown source. In some way it was confusing to me. So many people were cutting through the veil and becoming more and more conscious and empowered. Their problems were no longer problems for them, and their health and well-being were improving and expanding to levels we never dream of. Yet other people that were doing their process with the same, or even more, commitment were still creating, attracting, and experiencing pain in their lives. The patterns of behavior were repeating themselves. They kept complaining and biting upon themselves. Each session was like we were starting from scratch and I had the certainty that we were running in circles!

Because of my experience, I knew that underneath those layers of pain, there was something that was essentially their core of well-being or the light body: the original design, a place made of love, freedom, peace, and joy. I knew that these people had it, but what was preventing them from living their life from that place like the rest of the others doing the PBR process?

I started paying attention to the way they were expressing themselves and realized that they were believing in certain things that were creating pain and affecting their life perception. I realized that some of those beliefs were unconscious assumptions that told them who they were and what life was, or should be, for them. I knew that if I deeply believe that nobody loves me I would probably feel an undercurrent of sadness and fear in me, regardless of how much I accomplish or how great my life is at the moment.

Knowing that underneath all pain there is the joy body, I started asking seemingly silly questions like: "Is there anything good in feeling that sadness?" or, "What is the good side of feeling anxious?" or, "If there is any benefit in feeling rage, what is it?"

To my surprise, the answers to the puzzle were coming out of their own mouths without any effort in what I called a chain of beliefs, each link of the chain a belief the person learned in their formative years. They would say: "The benefit of being anxious is that I am more productive." *And the benefit of that?* "Is that I feel more responsible." *And the benefit of that?* "Is that I am a better father." *And the benefit of that?* "Is that I feel worthy." *And the benefit of that?* "Is that I can be more calm and relaxed."

As I said before, all these unconscious assumptions, or inner decisions, condition us to act or perform in a certain way that is no longer authentic or genuine to us. We create a self-image to adapt to the circumstances around us, trying to be included and accepted by the people we have to deal with.

I could see that the more we believe in an unconscious belief, the more we activate the self-image or the false persona. We become that belief. The more we live our lives from a false place, the less real and authentic life we have. We've been designed to be authentic and real, and the less real we are, the more contractions happen in our system. The more contractions we have in us, the larger the pain body grows. And the larger the pain body is, the smaller our light body is. As a consequence, we may experience more suffering and less joy and peace in our lives.

For example, when I subconsciously believe that I am unworthy and nobody loves me, I feel sad, alone, and afraid. When I feel this way, I may feel nervous and insecure. When I feel like that, I may say yes when I want to say no to people, trying to get them to like me. When I do that, I may resent others or even myself for doing what I don't want to do. Then I may feel anger and resentment, convinced that I have to attack, defend, and protect myself. Then nobody loves me, not even me! I judge and criticize myself and feel unworthy, and the cycle goes on and on and on.

Coming from the journey into the pain body, we can explore the unconscious beliefs that create the contractions. And coming from a more mental investigation, we can foresee the pain that is created as a result of having an unconscious belief. What I like about NNR is that everyone can run their own neural pathways without anyone doing it for them. And once you learn how to do it, you can run multiple chains of beliefs, and that gets really exciting! The CMR facilitators teach it to our clients and after few sessions they do it without any of our help.

There are three main goals in doing NNR:

1. Uncover the unconscious assumptions and the links between the beliefs.
2. Bring light to the roots and deepest causes if needed.
3. Deactivate the assumptions and the chain of beliefs created unconsciously.

1. Uncover the unconscious assumptions and the links between the beliefs.

   We become aware of the whole neuropathway, looking for the benefits with presence and the curiosity of a child.

2. Bring light to the roots and deepest causes if needed.

   Sometimes becoming aware of the circumstances that originated the unconscious assumptions is crucial. Even though in CMR the story is mostly irrelevant, bringing light onto the cause of the wound can be the catalyst for great transformation. As children we created a self-image based on very important assumptions and decisions following what was going on then. Getting to know the neuropathway is the beginning, but is not enough to deactivate the pattern. After reading the chain of beliefs backward a few times to bring awareness, we may ask ourselves some questions like: Do I recognize this pattern? Is it familiar to me? How does it affect my life? Where is this coming from? Where did I learn it? What's the earliest memory I have of having it? Is there anything that led me to believe this? Who else was involved in this experience? As the file starts opening, we will find what unconscious assumptions we made inside our mind at that early age.

3. Deactivate the assumptions and the chain of beliefs created unconsciously.

   Once we find the origin, and the unconscious connections that support the beliefs, we ask ourselves some questions to verify if we want to keep believing it, or we choose not to.

   a. Is this belief true? Is it real? Is it something I would teach to a child as a teaching for life?

   b. How do I feel when I believe it?

   c. Does anyone benefit from it? A real, genuine benefit?

   d. What would my life be like if I no longer maintain this belief? What would my words or actions be like if I no longer believe them?

In what follows, I'll present some real cases in which the NNR technique was used. These people took the CMR process for the first time. The NNR approach tries to find the benefit underlying the experienced negative state and allows the healing and transformation of the underlying pattern. I suggest that, after reading each case, you take a piece of paper and a pencil, and write down those neural pathways you have discovered that produce in you unnecessary suffering. Also journal about any beliefs you discover that negate the truth of whom you really are. You may be amazed and liberated by what you discover.

Neural pathway #1
Client: a woman, forty-five years old
Presenting problem: *She had been diagnosed with clinical depression and declared disabled many years ago. She had been taking pills for depression and anxiety for around fifteen years. She reported the following:* "During the day, I feel weak most of the time, and I can't sleep well at night. I always get up in the morning feeling tired. I get tired even with the smallest activity. I feel I'm a burden to my relatives, since I completely depend on them. I'm useless."

Questions to find the polarity
Q: *What is it that you don't want to feel?*
A: "I don't want to feel weak, tired, depressed."
Q: *In a perfect world, how would you feel?*
A: "I want to feel strong. I'd like to have more joy!"

Questions to find the benefits
I decided to begin the work with the word "weak," since the person had often used it in her descriptions of her situation.

Q: *What would be the benefit, the positive side, of feeling weak?*
A: "That everybody must pay attention to me."

Q: *What is the benefit of them paying attention to you? What is the positive side of it?*

A: "That they worry about me."

Q: *What is the benefit of them worrying about you, the positive side of it?*

A: "That I feel I'm being pampered."

Q: *What is the benefit of being pampered?*

A: "That I feel loved."

Q: *What is the positive side of it?*

A: "That I feel more joy and alive."

Q: *What is the benefit of feeling more joy and alive, the positive side of it?*

A: "That I feel more strong and energetic."

Some people initially find it almost impossible to believe that they derive any benefit from the negative state of their situation. If this happens to you, don't be alarmed. It may help to ask yourself, *If I have to explain to a martian who has just landed on Earth what the benefits of being depressed are, what would I say?* or *If this was happening to someone you know, what benefits might I see?*

Feedback on the neural pathway

Once this information is organized, I read the person what the pathway tells, back and forth, so as to generate potential associations and memories. I give her time to slowly listen and metabolize this information. This process usually triggers unexpected responses, such as uncontrolled laughter, sadness, skepticism, or shame. Each one of these relations has an origin and a story to be told. In the beginning, they appear as a result of painful experiences or by mere imitation. We call each of them a belief. Each belief is linked to the next one, and all of them together form a pathway of beliefs, or neural pathway. When any of the links of the pathway is stimulated by a given experience at the present moment, the pathway reacts as a whole.

The initial reading of the pathway:

To feel *strong*, I have to feel more *joy and alive*.

To feel more *joy and alive,* I have to *feel loved.*
To feel *loved,* I have to feel *pampered.*
To feel *pampered,* I have to feel that *people worry about me.*
To feel that *people worry about me,* I have to feel that *they are paying attention to me.*
And to feel that *they are paying attention to me,* I have to feel *weak.*

Another reading of this pathway:
To feel *strong,* I have to feel *more joy and alive.*
To feel *strong,* I have to feel *loved.*
To feel *strong,* I have to feel *pampered.*
To feel *strong,* I have to feel that *people worry about me.*
To feel *strong,* I have to feel that *people pay attention to me.*

And, as a consequence of all the above:
To feel *strong,* I have to feel *weak.*

The same procedure can be followed with each of the feelings mentioned:

To feel more *joy and alive,* I have to feel *loved.*
To feel more *joy and alive,* I have to feel *pampered.*
To feel more *joy and alive,* I have to feel that *people worry about me.*
To feel more *joy and alive,* I have to feel that *people pay attention to me.*
And to feel more *joy and alive,* I have to feel *weak.*

Discovering the original wound
When I asked the person, "Where do you think all this comes from?" she took some time to think and then told me the following:

- When she was young, she was quite inquisitive and passionate. She played and behaved "almost like a boy" and couldn't stay quiet.

- Her mother, her father, and her sister got angry with her daily because, they said, "she was out of control." She was very frequently criticized, and this made her feel judged, despised, and not loved.
- Her sister was the favorite daughter and always got the best grades at school, being rewarded by their parents with gifts, trips, and a better education.
- My client only remembered two times in her childhood when she felt loved and pampered by her parents. The first one was when she was four and fell ill with pneumonia; the second one was when she was five and had an accident that prevented her from walking for several months. "I've never felt more loved in all my life!" she exclaimed.
- When she was ten years old, she already suffered from depression, as she later found out it was called.

Outlining the self-image

Some important parts of this woman's self-image were formed from decisions unconsciously made because of her need to be loved and to feel in touch with her closest relatives in her childhood. Decisions made at that early time are absolute for us and there is no choice to do anything different when we grow up. We could say that they are hardwired into our brain. What follows is a summary of the information collected throughout the session about decisions made at an early age and triggered after the accident she had when she was five.

How did you see yourself at that age? Do you have any idea about the "inner talk" of that five-year-old girl living in that family environment?
- "There's something bad in me."
- "Nobody loves me as I am."
- "I can't be myself."
- "When I become active and enjoy myself, nobody loves me."
- "To be loved, I must be calm and quiet."
- "Any time I feel strong, I get in trouble."
- "I do everything wrong."
- "People love me when I'm weak or when I'm ill."

Neural pathway #2

Client: a woman, thirty-five years old.

Presenting problem: "I have a very active and intense life, but I'm stressed and anxious most of the time. I'm always worrying about something. I get easily tired and wearied, but even so, I don't stop doing things. They tell me I'm always trying to control everything."

Questions to find the polarity

Q: *How do you not want to feel?*

A: "I don't want to feel anxious."

Q: *How do you want to feel?*

A: "I want to feel more relaxed and at peace. I want to feel more joy in life."

Questions to find the benefits

I began the inquiry with the word "anxious."

Q: *What would be the benefit, the positive side, of feeling anxious?*

A: "That I'm on the alert and on guard."

Q: *What is the benefit of being on the alert and on guard, the positive side of it?*

A: "That I feel prepared and protected."

Q: *What is the positive side of being prepared and protected?*

A: "That I feel more calm and safe."

Q: *What is the benefit of feeling more calm and safe, the positive side of it?*

A: "That I feel at peace."

Paradoxically to feel at peace, you have to feel anxious.

Discovering the original wound

The person immediately remembered that:

- When she was four, her mother was admitted into a psychiatric hospital. My client was present when her mother was taken away. Her mother never came back home.

- My client was the eldest of three siblings.
- Her father was a drug addict and an alcoholic. She remembered that he often left her and her siblings alone and without food for several days.

Outlining the self-image
How did you see yourself at that age? Do you have any idea about the "inner talk" of that four-year-old girl living through those experiences?
- "I can't trust anyone."
- "If I don't do things, nobody will do them."
- "I have to manage all by myself."
- "I will never be able to have children." [She actually had not had any.]
- "Men are irresponsible."
- "I can't trust them."
- "They are weak, selfish, and foolish."

Neural pathway #3
Client: a man, thirty-six years old
Presenting problem: "I'm quite sensitive to criticism; I take it as a personal attack. I react defensively and get very irritated. This affects all my relationships, especially at my job, because I work in a team with other people. When they object to something I do, I get mad. I have chronic digestive problems, mainly when I eat a lot of sweets or smoke marijuana. When this happens, I feel guilty and sad, but I can't stop doing it."

Questions to find the polarity
Q: *How do you least want to feel?*
A: "I don't want to feel ill. I don't want to be irritated all the time."
Q: *What would you really like to feel?*
A: "I want to feel relaxed. I want to feel more joy."

Questions to find the benefits

I began the inquiry with the word "irritated."

Q: *What would be the benefit, the positive side, of being irritated?*

A: "That I feel justified."

Q: *What would be the positive side of feeling justified?*

A: "That I feel that people listen to me."

Q: *What would be the positive side of being listened to?*

A: "That I feel important and valued."

Q: *What would be the positive side of feeling important and valued?*

A: "That I feel approved."

Q: *What would be the positive side of feeling approved?*

A: "That I can relax and be myself."

So, in order to relax and be myself, I need to feel irritated.

Discovering the original wound

The person reported that:
- When he was a child, his mother was a fault-finder, a perfectionist who always remarked that something hadn't been done right or was "unfinished."
- He never felt that his achievements were recognized.
- Often, his mother berated him in front of other people.
- His mother never admitted her own mistakes and never apologized for her own faults.
- His father permanently complained about everything and hid himself so as not to be criticized by her. When he was discovered in some wrongdoing, he got angry and defended himself desperately.

Outlining the self-image

How did you see yourself at that age? Have you any idea about the "inner talk" of that boy living through those experiences?
- "No matter what I do, it's never enough."
- "I'm weak and helpless."

- "I must hide."
- "I'm a loser."
- "Nothing I do has value or meaning."
- "I do everything wrong."
- "Sweets make me feel better."

Neural pathway #4

Client: a woman, twenty-nine years old

Presenting problem: *She has compulsively plucked and torn out her eyebrow hairs and eyelashes since she was in kindergarten. Her mother would get very angry with her because of this. Very often, this caused infections and it was all quite disagreeable. She has been taking antidepressants since she was twenty-one years old. She reports the following:* "I feel weak and horrible. I don't want to approach anybody lest they realize what I have done to my face. I do the same with the small hairs that grow on my legs. I wear long trousers so nobody can see them. I avoid showing my body and going to places where I must undress. I feel weak and helpless. I should have already overcome this foolish thing. People have real problems, and they overcome them. In my case, I've begun different treatments, but nothing changed. I have no control over this and I'm in despair!"

Questions to find the polarity

Q: *How do you not want to feel?*

A: "I don't want to feel weak and helpless."

Q: *How do you want to feel?*

A: "I want to feel strong. I want to feel joy in my life."

Questions to find the benefits

I began the inquiry with the word "weak."

Q: *What would be the benefit, the positive side, of being weak?*

A: "That they worry about me."

Q: *What would be the positive side of them worrying about you?*

A: "That people care about me."

Q: *What would be the positive side of people caring about you?*
A: "That I feel loved, accepted, and respected."
Q: *What would be the positive side of feeling loved, accepted, and respected?*
A: "That I feel I'm beautiful."
Q: *What would be the positive side of feeling beautiful?*
A: "That I can increase my self-trust."
Q: *What would be the positive side of increasing your self-trust?*
A: "That I feel strong and at peace with myself."

In this case, in order to feel strong and at peace with myself, you need to feel weak.

Discovering the original wound
After the neural pathway was fed back to her, the person shared that:
- She has a younger brother that has always been very weak and sickly, while she was always healthy and attractive.
- Her brother had been born through a forceps delivery when she was three years old. As a result, he had malformations of the skull and was mentally retarded. The mother stayed several weeks at the hospital caring for him after the birth.
- Meanwhile, she was taken to a grandmother's home for several months. No one told her anything. She didn't know what was going on. From then on, her relationship with her mother was never the same as before.

Outlining the self-image
Some of the decisions made by my client at three years old, after her brother's birth, were the following:
- "There's something wrong with me. That's why they no longer love me."
- "I'm not important."
- "I'm a dead loss."
- "They love you when you're weak."
- "They like you and care for you when you're ugly."
- "Everyone that loves me quits without warning."

- "Everything I do, I do wrong."
- "They will always reject me."

People are often stunned to realize how much their lives have been twisted and altered by these seemingly absurd neuropathways. It is usually easy for them to recognize the origin of the patterns in their lives, and they may experience great relief when they realize they can deactivate these patterns. By bringing awareness to these neural pathways and the false beliefs in them, they begin to dissolve, creating more energy, leading to greater authenticity and joy.

EXERCISE

1. Run your own neuropathway.
2. Explore the issue and feelings, and find the benefits.
3. Write down the issue on a piece of paper.
4. What do you feel when you think about it? Write it down. (Choose one feeling if you wrote more than one. Start with the most charged feeling.)
5. Ask yourself: *What is the benefit of feeling* _____? (If the answer is an action, ask yourself how you feel when you do that. Also, make sure that it is a real benefit. For example, "Then I get to hate myself" is not a benefit. "Then I don't have to feel responsible" is a genuine benefit.)
6. Repeat question 5 to build the neural pathway until you reach the deepest positive feeling.
7. Read back the neural pathway starting from the positive feeling and working backward using all the words in it: "In order to _____ I need to _____."
8. Ask yourself: *Is this pattern familiar to me or currently active in my life? Where did I learn this belief? Is this belief 100 percent true? Would I teach this belief to a child? How do I feel when I believe this? Does anybody truly benefit when I believe this? What would my life be like if I don't believe this? Am I willing to drop this belief?*

To get free access to more exercises like this one, please go to: www.cellularmemory.org

MEMORY IN THE CELLS

There is a saying that simple awareness is often curative, meaning that by simply bringing attention to something, it often begins to heal. Seeing the neural nets in your life will begin to break the neural connections and initiate transformation. One way to think of it is that as you do PBR, you are taking out the trash, or clearing any blockages in your energy system like when unplugging a stuck pipe. By examining your beliefs, your self-images, your neural nets, you are making sure that the pipes do not plug back up, that no more trash enters your system.

The result? To genuinely heal something from the inside out. Yes, the process may take more time and commitment than you may expect. Yet consider the worth of experiencing lasting peace, freedom, and love.

An Invitation

Our birth is but a sleep and a forgetting:
The Soul that rises with us, our life's Star,
Hath had elsewhere its setting,
And cometh from afar.
Not in entire forgetfulness, and not in utter nakedness,
But trailing clouds of glory do we come
From God, who is our home:
Heaven lies about us in our infancy!
—William Wordsworth

Many people feel a deep sense of happiness or connection when in the presence of an infant. It is easy to see babies as loving and blissful. Yet how easy is it to recognize this same essence in an adult? As time passes, that inner light seems to diminish and fade; the "clouds of glory" appear extinguished by doubt, judgment, fear, and other negative conditioning we received inadvertently from our parents, teachers, friends, and lovers. Yet regardless of how dim that light becomes, our truth is joy, peace, and love. For many of us, no matter how much we yearn for these qualities, nothing could feel further from the truth. A state of anxiety or depression pervades many of us. It is easier to believe that "life is suffering" than it is to believe that we are joy.

Humankind is developing more and more effective ways to return to the truth of our innate nature, thankfully. The CMR process is one of these pathways, undergoing constant transformation to meet the ever-shifting needs of humanity during this time of great evolution. It is as mysterious as life itself. But at the same time humankind is creating its own healing opportunities, it is also developing more ways to harm each other. Which will we choose? By liberating ourselves from the "story" of our problems and entering the moment-to-moment physical responses to our feelings, thoughts, and emotions, a portal in our own bodies leads us back to our essential nature as divine intelligence, the same intelligence that runs the entire universe. In this place, the inevitable transformation and healing of even the most painful or immutable challenges is relatively rapid. For those who despair that they will never heal their deep wounds and experience peace and joy, there is hope. In our cynical world, this probably seems hard to believe. Don't take anyone's word for it. Be like the Buddha who cautioned his followers not to believe anything he said but rather to check their own experience. Try it for yourself so you too can have the direct experience of a profound transformation and joy. The only thing you have to lose is suffering.

The Opportunity Is Yours for the Taking

When we transform our inner world, our outer world naturally changes without us having to even try. Our inner world functions as a magnet drawing to us events in our outer world. For this to happen, one needs to work from the inside out. The CMR process does exactly that. The pain body, which is inside each one of us, stores, circulates, and recycles negative emotional charge (NEC) automatically throughout our bodies, creating a toxic "bad feeling" effect. Eckhart Tolle, renowned author of *The Power of Now* and *A New Earth*, speaks about the pain body as an entity unto itself that prevents us from knowing whom or what we really are. We couldn't have given the stored negative emotional charge in us a better name or a more accurate definition than Eckhart Tolle's.

My experience working with thousands of people have shown me that:

(1) the pain body can be released, and peace and well-being can be attained through the awakening of the light body.

(2) we can effectively deal with and transform ongoing life difficulties without creating drama and storing additional pain in our bodies.

(3) we need to deactivate the underlying belief system that supports and fuels the discomfort in us so that permanent, beneficial shifts in awareness and well-being can occur.

The more we do the CMR process, the more it deepens and becomes a part of who we are. Learning how to do it requires un-learning what we know in order to make space for the new and remembering what we have forgotten—our innate ability to transform discomfort into peace … separation into connection … inner fragmentation into integration and well-being. Armed with this process, we can stop the cycle we were taught, first within ourselves, and naturally extend it outward to create the world we really want for ourselves and those who follow. Truly, we can create a new earth.

Get the Support and Containment You Need

Take a moment to think about all the influences you are under and how they may be affecting your life on different levels. The conditioning that runs deep in your genetic code, the cultural education and family influences that you have received, can be transformed through structured, disciplined, and conscious action and investigation. In this way any individual who is willing to take responsibility for his life is able to dismantle it and experience freedom and inner peace.

There are several options to help you gain momentum beyond this book. Because of the nature of this work, a comfortable, supportive, neutral, and empathic environment—whether online, over the phone, or in person—is absolutely necessary. You may be interested in attending or referring someone to any of the live events that are being offered to support and add to what you've learned up to this point.

Nothing spreads a good thing better than word of mouth and personal, direct experience. We are all swimming in the same ocean, so the more we can support this new direction and develop a new habit toward empowerment and awareness, the more it benefits all of us. Here are some of the resources that we have created that are available to you. Some of them are absolutely free of charge:

Free CMR eSeries on Emotional Healing at the Cellular Level
These are practical lessons with steps and valuable exercises to trigger the process of transformation and healing in ourselves and others. After enrolling, you will receive them in your inbox once a week.
http://www.cellularmemory.org/index_english.php

Recourses for Self-Transformation
You may be interested in ordering books, e-books or the DVD's with recorded CMR events. In this way you can experience them from the privacy of your home and watch them at your own pace.
http://www.cellularmemory.org/products/products.html

Free Tele-Seminars (phone)
These activities over the phone are for you if you want to know more about CMR, share your own experiences, and ask me your questions.

There are many aspects of daily life that we cover in a tele-seminar, and I enjoy sharing how the combination of the CMR tools can create healing and transformation no matter what challenge you are facing. They are usually one hour in length. Check out the current schedule in the following link:

http://www.cellularmemory.org/activities/activities_telebridges.php

Web Classes (Internet)

Thanks to modern technology and the Internet, we have the ability to interact with the readers and teach through a series of Web classes that I have put together over the years. It doesn't matter where you are on the planet. As long as you have a good Internet connection and speakers, you will be able to get all the insights as if we were in the same room together. These classes are for those who value the ease of learning from their home and who are interested in learning the basics and application of the CMR process. Check out our current schedule of Web classes below:

http://www.cellularmemory.org/activities/activities_webclasses.php

Live Events for Personal Development

These activities happen in places where I am traveling or where there are local CMR facilitators available. To find out the location and the dates available go to:

http://www.cellularmemory.org/activities/activities.php

Personal or Phone Coaching CMR Sessions

A CMR session is unique and unfolds in the moment. I frequently say to the people interested in taking sessions that this work is meant to be practical. Therefore I ask them to avoid bringing intellectual or philosophical discussions, which only will stimulate more the logical mind and frequently create confusion. If you are just curious or you have the desire to discuss the theory behind this work, the private sessions are not the place for it. There is plenty of information being offered in this book, through tele-seminars, DVD's, and CD's, and in the CMR Web site: www.cellularmemory.org

During these sessions, you will be guided to connect deeply with your body and yourself. Gradually, that will expose the cellular memory programming, the belief patterns, and the self-image you still cling to, which prevents you from healing and realizing the truth about yourself. In those inner places, you will find the main obstacles that prevent you from accessing your unlimited potential for peace, freedom, and joy in the present moment. If you want to know more or if you have any questions prior to booking your sessions, you can request a twenty-minute free consultation going to the link below.

http://www.cellularmemory.org/privatesessions/privatesessions.html

CMR Trainings

If you are interested in applying this process to yourself, you can take the CMR training and if you are interested in applying it to others, then become a facilitator in Cellular Memory Release. In order to be a facilitator, you will have to practice to gain ease, confidence, and experience in combining and applying the techniques successfully with clients or friends. This training takes about eighteen to twenty four months to complete and is a combination of live events and tele-seminars with practice and supervision. The CMR training is offered in different locations and in different languages. Check our site for dates and more details:

http://www.cellularmemory.org/activities/activities_cmrtraining.php

Free Videos, Forums, and Blogs on CMR

With the help of several CMR facilitators, we created a free membership site where members can participate with their questions and contributions. There you will find past tele-seminars, videos, and blogs in both Spanish and English languages.

www.cellularmemory.org

Looking forward to sharing with you any of these resources!

In awareness and healing,

Luis Diaz

REFERENCES AND SUGGESTED READING

Chamberlin, David. *The Mind of Your Newborn Baby.* Berkeley: North Atlantic Books, 1998.

Grabhorn, Lynn. *Excuse Me, Your Life Is Waiting.* Charlottesville, Virginia: Hampton Roads Publishing Co. 2001.

Katie, Byron. *Loving What Is: Four Questions That Can Change Your Life.* New York: Three Rivers Press 2002.

Lipton, Bruce. *The Biology of Belief: Unleashing the Power of Unconsciousness, Matter, and Miracles.* Santa Rosa: Ingram, Baker & Taylor 2005.

Pearsall, Paul. *The Heart's Code: Tapping the Wisdom and Power of Our Heart Energy.* New York: Broadway Books 1998.

Pert, Candace. *Molecules of Emotion: Why You Feel the Way You Feel.* New York: Touchstone 1999.

Tolle, Eckhart. *A New Earth: Awakening to Your Life's Purpose.* New York: Penguin 2008.

Tolle, Eckhart. *The Power of Now.* Novato, CA: New World Library 1999.

Verny, Thomas. *The Secret Life of the Unborn Child.* New York: Summit Books 1981.

Made in the USA
Middletown, DE
01 April 2019